JULIETTE STAPLETON

# ON MARKETING & HUMAN DESIGN

EMBODY YOUR TRUE SELF & RECLAIM YOUR POWER FOR MAGNETIC ONLINE VISIBILITY

FOREWORD BY MARI SMITH

ISBN: 978-9916-4-1898-7



Author's website: https://juliettestapleton.com

**Further resources for readers: https://marketingbyhumandesign.com**

Book Cover by Juliette Stapelton

Book Cover by Juliette Stapelton

Supported by: AMA Publishing, https://amapublishing.co

1st Edition edition 2023

**Behind this woman stood a man that believed in her**.

He did not want to think about his imminent end, even when saying goodbyes. "*I like you "in the zone". Don't you dare ever give it up*", he said...

To Les Stapleton (1959-2023)

Thank you for the music...

# Contents

# Foreword by Mari Smith

## It's Time To Shine Your Light!

There's a myth out there in the world of marketing. Most entrepreneurs somehow learn that the way to market themselves is with *great force*. You've probably heard these mantras of marketing gurus: *'Hustle and grind!' 'Push yourself hard!' 'Beat the competition!' 'Amass as many followers as you can because everyone knows it's a numbers game!'*

But this style of marketing is simply *not* correctly aligned with the vast majority of business owners around the world, hence they struggle and feel frustrated. So many people have bought into this mad rush and are caught up in the daily hamster wheel of trying to prove themselves, borrowing other people's methods to no avail.

The thing is, we are ALL uniquely and beautifully different. We are here to shine our light, to live out our life's purpose, and to express our differentiated genetic imprint in a very specific way. There is a reason Human Design is referred to as 'the Science of Differentiation.' Nobody on the planet is as unique as you. Even identical twins have slightly different and unique genetic imprints.

When you discover how to market in correct alignment with your True Self, it can literally make or break your business. In her delightful new book, Juliette Stapleton has done a remarkable job of breaking down the most important aspects of the Human Design System and explaining them in understandable terms. She gives you exactly what you need to apply this profound body of work to effectively develop your brand and correctly market yourself, sell your services, and grow your business.

The Human Design System is needed now more than ever, *especially* in the business world. Not just having your chart run and knowing a few distinctions. But really, truly understanding the fundamentals in a way that you're empowered with practical applications in your life and business.

Everyone has a personal brand. One of the biggest buzzwords since the beginning of social media's prevalence (circa 2006) is 'Authenticity.' In his book *Tribes: We Need You To Lead Us*, that came out in 2008, renowned marketing author and leader, Seth Godin, stated *"People can smell the agenda of a leader."*

When you put yourself out there correctly – in alignment with your true self – people can sense, see, and feel your authentic intent. The right people are more likely to respond favorably to you in a way that is correctly aligned within themselves.

Conversely, when you are misaligned within yourself, and you're using marketing methods that are simply not a fit, your audience can also sense that. They're more likely to feel discordant energy and not necessarily gravitate towards you.

We talk about the deconditioning process in Human Design. I like to think of this as Michelangelo chipping away at a big lump of marble in front of him and revealing the statue of David. The more conscious we can become of our Not-Self 'monkey mind' and 'chip away at it,' the more we can allow our *true nature* to shine through. This is authenticity. This is what you want to portray in your marketing efforts: your own, unique expression in the world.

Juliette is uniquely equipped to bring you these teachings through her powerful new book. Her passion and depth of knowledge of Human Design, along with her experience and practical application in the world of marketing, shines through every page. As a Projector (Advisor in BG5 terms), Juliette is definitely here to guide the energy of others. She is an inspiring agent with depth, talent, and influence. Her logical, no-nonsense approach to creating lasting visibility through embodying Human Design is a joy to read.

As a fellow 1/3, I definitely relate to Juliette's Public Role in life. Deeply investigative (with ten Line 1's!), I love to get to the bottom line, create a solid foundation, and only then share with the world what I've discovered when I feel secure that I've become an authority. And, oh my, that unconscious trial and error process as a pioneer! I've always considered myself very resilient and am not afraid to try new things.

I've been a top social media thought leader, specializing in Facebook marketing, since 2007. My community gave me the moniker 'the Queen of Facebook.' Specializing in Facebook, with its constant changes and challenges, certainly keeps me on my toes and satisfies my first and third line processes. (In fact, as a third line, my social media career for 16+ years is the longest I've ever stuck with any one path, given there is so much variety!)

It was right at the beginning of my Facebook marketing career that Juliette first started following me. Over the years, we had a few brief DM exchanges. Fast forward to January 2023: I had just shared a podcast interview on my Facebook profile where I talked about my passion for the Human Design System, and the fact I was in my third year of studies to become a certified professional analyst with the International Human Design School.

Juliette reached out to me with great enthusiasm and invited me to be a guest on her podcast. We have since had many wonderful, in-depth exchanges sharing our passion and geeking out on all things Human Design. My Sacral responded with such a positive buzz when Juliette graciously asked me if I would like to write the Foreword for her new book.

I actually had my very first Human Design foundational reading in the early 2000's when I was in a whole other career. But it wasn't until Winter Solstice 2020 when a dear friend came over to my house for a visit. She told me, *"Mari, as I was walking out the door this morning, my intuition told me to grab this book off the shelf and bring it to you."* She pulled the book out. It was a book on Human Design.

My whole body buzzed with excitement. I threw my arms in the air and practically jumped out of my seat. *"WHAT?!! Human Design?!! There are books on that? You can study it?"* I heard myself saying. Ha! As a Pure Sacral Generator, I came to learn that was a solid benchmark for my Sacral Response, my Inner Authority.

Human Design has made such a tremendous impact on my personal relationships and in my business world. Understanding the genetic imprints of my loved ones, clients, and team members has really helped me to grok how radically different we each are and to simply allow them to be. And, what a difference to trust my Sacral response vs. trying to initiate and be a 'go-getter' all the time.

Whatever your own Type, Strategy and Authority, my wish for you is that you'll dive deep into this profound work with great gusto – as is correct for you – through Juliette's amazing book.

The world needs your authentic, true self now more than ever. It's time to shine your light as powerfully as you can. There's no better system to aid you in becoming all you can be in your business and personal life than the Human Design System. And, with Juliette as your guide, the sky is the limit!

With much love from my heart to yours,

Mari Smith

Social Media Through Leader, Premier Facebook Marketing Expert, Author, *The New Relationship Marketing* (Wiley 2011)

Ashland, Oregon, USA

# Ink and Intention

## Unmasking the Vision

I am a Splenic Projector 1/3. If you are new to Human Design, this sounds like complete gibberish to you. But by the end of this book (and you do not have to read everything in this book), my goal is to give you invaluable insight to add to your awareness and understanding of how your unique energies work. I will also show you how you can use this awareness to re-align your business with WHO you are and what you are about when living your true potential.

What you are reading is not a textbook on Human Design, or marketing for that matter. Much of what you will read combines my visibility strategist experience and obsession with the Human Design system. The knowledge that opened "the door" to a deep understanding of how we show up, bond, and interact. It explained why some things do not work for some people. Just as most traditional marketing advice does not work for a solopreneur who is a coach, a spiritual worker, a digital creator, and many more, to be frank. I happily walked through that door, and I continue diving deeper and deeper into that knowledge every day.

But in this book, I want to keep it light and to the point for you. I will assume you know nothing (or not much) about Human Design or marketing to keep it very easy to understand.

I hope to enlighten you on how Human Design helps you make reliable, correct decisions in your life and business. I want to empower you in how your True Self shows up in your life and describe how others perceive and connect to you so that you can align your decisions and your strategies to what is more CORRECT. I also want to help you find harmony within and attract the most amazing people - the ones that you will LOVE to have around- as they help you feel amazing within yourself while you are aligning more and more with your purpose, feeling fulfilled in how you help others, and creating the life of your dreams.

I am not afraid to use clichés here because I am typing this from a cosy apartment in the city centre of the medieval city of Tallinn, Estonia - looking out on the most energetically aligned place in the world (for me, of course). It is the area I dreamed of living in as a child, with the tall spears of the medieval old town at a distance. In this very energetically special place, the ancient stones in the streets and buildings have always given me a sense of complete grounding and openness to receive abundance.

This was my biggest desire in life at the start of 2017 - a vague dream of wanting to be where I feel aligned. Now, it is a kind of mundane everyday reality, and I have to remind myself that things were very different only a few years back.

The even more ironic fact? Tallinn is my hometown.

I emigrated from here in 1999 following the calling to "go West" to find my other half. And I did. Perhaps this is a story for another book, with a bold journey of following another dream and doing whatever it took. This included taking a solo bus journey from London to Dublin, Ireland, eight months pregnant with a suitcase and nobody on the other side, just to ensure the baby was born in a Western country that we could legally base ourselves on and build that life of our dreams.

And how the baby was indeed born there, and I called Ireland my home for two decades to follow.

My daughter still lives in Dublin. She is a Scholar at Trinity College Dublin and an already published (at the age of 20) theoretical physicist in the middle of her PhD studies. This is one of the intricate reasons I had to spend 20 years in a place utterly misaligned with who I was; the climate, the culture, and the people. All except just a few - my other half, whom I met in Dublin in 2003, and a couple of very dear-to-me clients who, over time, grew into my "Irish family."

Still, a few people out of over five million (if we take into consideration the whole population of Ireland) isn't much. In fact, after coming back 20 years later, I feel like it never even happened. Only memories of events remained, but no connection. The way the mind works is often so strange.

In another story, back in Ireland in April 2017, there was this wake-up call when my husband Les got sick and diagnosed with very aggressive stage IV Lymphoma cancer -just three weeks before we were finally getting married (and after 13 years of engagement). His medical history still contains a note from a doctor about getting everything they could to help him "walk the aisle" on his wedding day. It reminds me of one of our favourite movies, *"Only You"*, where the Italians stop the plane so the heroine can catch up with the one she loved. I love these synchronicities in life, messages that come to us through other stories that we later experience in our lives...

You see, in my life, ALL my dreams have come true. My challenge has been to adjust to the "happily ever after" and build more dreams. It is more complex than it sounds. Sometimes it takes a severe blow in your face...

When Les got sick in 2017, I made the most unexpected decision -

to follow my calling. I decided to focus on a point way beyond his recovery. I focused on the dreams we had and being in a place that is correct for us on every level - living a lifestyle that feels sweet and warm – especially indoors. If you ever lived long-term in the UK and Ireland, you know what I am talking about, and this was definitely a very incorrect factor for me.

I embarked on a journey with that focused vision. It was an unexpected and unusual journey in our circumstances. Still, I channelled all my energy into creating flexibility and freedom from location and face-to-face commitments to clients in my business.

I threw myself into creating an online coaching business and marketing myself. I was showing up as the face of my business and using all my skills, knowledge, and expertise to figure out how I could attract clients and, more importantly - truly ideal clients - into my business without any geographic constraints, so I could live anywhere and still continue attracting prosperity and abundance through my business. I set an intention for my business to be able to support the life we would love to live every day.

**My life today...**

I have had the honour to mentor and coach clients worldwide: from Chile to Nova Scotia, from Singapore to Texas, and even a Russian digital nomad living in Vanuatu! I have retained some fantastic clients for years. As I unlock my true purpose, more and more aligned beautiful souls allow me to open this door and show them what is possible when they let their True Selves emerge and guide them through their online visibility, business decisions, attracting, and, more importantly, CHOOSING who to work with, and really every other aspect of their lives.

This is what I intend for you.

And Les? Miraculously, in 2017 his treatment worked, and he enjoyed his life with me to the full without any health concerns for over five years (apart from that one time we all got Covid in 2022, but then it was really inevitable at some point). And I don't want to claim that "I did it," - but I know that focusing on the point way beyond the issue at hand (his recovery) definitely worked. And I am so eternally grateful.

What you are reading right now is about me, although this book will be all about you at the end of the day. I would love you to treat this book as a reference - and when we go into the "meat and potatoes," only read what applies to you. However, if stories of my life and examples from my relationships with clients and people, in general, will help illustrate how transformational this direction is, I would be humbly grateful.

As I wrote this book, my husband's Lymphoma cancer came back out of nowhere. It attacked his nervous system and his brain. The start of 2023 marked the most emotionally painful period in my life. At this time, we had to slowly start saying goodbye to everything we shared together as the disease began chipping away at his memories, abilities to write, and then read. Our grief started weeks before we had to say the final farewell on the morning of St. Patrick's Day.

He took his last breath in my arms. Loved.

One thing that comforts me is that, no matter how cruelly this disease affected his mind, he had me in focus until that last moment - of that, I am sure. I was his life. The love of his life. And he was mine - and nothing could take this away from us. That experience of bonding -love and grief, in sickness and in health, for better or for worse - those vowels are, in fact, part of my Design. I am here to master the consciousness of bonding and teach it to others...

In the rare lucid moments before his death, Les always told me so many things that gave me a sense of closure while our karmic contract was ending. He also told me to focus on *"staying in my zone*". Even when I had to tell him his condition was most likely terminal, he immediately replied about me, *"I like you in the zone,*" looking at the tears falling down my face as I was trying to get a grip on my emotions. *"The zone?*" I was confused...

*"Yes, I love when you are inspired and do what you do. I see a huge growth curve ahead of you. Don't you dare give up on it - you are brilliant...*" he replied.

Both Splenic Projectors, my husband Les, and I discovered "life in the moment" on a completely different level. For my husband, whose brain was attacked by cancer, it was the tricky memory distortion, and there were days when the only time he truly knew was right there in the moment. Everything else was a blur. Many critical traumatic events (like losing his parents) were erased from his memory entirely. Every 10 minutes, he forgot what had just happened. When he remembered some things, it was like a ray of sunshine on a rainy day, and those days were the days we said all the good stuff we needed to say to each other, all the things that mattered. Love and devotion to each other forever. Gratitude.

And for me, the challenge was to stay in the moment without being pulled into the past or the future, so I could be there, present for him in the hospital whenever they let me (the Covid restrictions forbade all hospital visits at the time - it was a constant struggle to get permission to see him). I also had to learn to be much more present for my daughter, who dealt with her anxiety at home.

And, of course, it was the time in my life when I had to learn how to be fully present with my Splenic KNOWING.

I had the "knowing" that this time we were not facing a recovery, as well as somewhere deep down, knowing that this would inevitably become another springboard in my life.

Just like first cancer in 2017 started my online business journey and created the life of our dreams, I learned to surrender to knowing that when the time comes, I will be able to soar even further and realise my potential as a thought leader, an advisor, and someone who is on a mission to contribute to a better world, better businesses, and better lives...

This is what helped me finish this book. With every word I write, I am eternally grateful to my husband, lover, best friend, and forever mentor, Les Stapleton, for giving me his blessing and letting me do this.

It took just two fast-paced months, with a rollercoaster of shock, disbelief, sorrow, reflection, anger, desperation, and finally, surrender. The moment Les died was the most beautiful, peaceful experience I have witnessed, despite being the most painful memory I must carry for the rest of my days.

When I met Les, I knew he was here to bring me to the other "shore"- to show me the way and help me find myself. He was a music producer and one of the most talented Ireland has ever seen. He was also incredibly influential as a mentor and music technology educator. His alumni are so impressive. His students produced names like Michael Jackson, Snow Patrol, The Script, and R.E.M. I was also one of his students at one time, experiencing his outstanding guidance firsthand.

Little did I know that he was going to become THE ONE that GUIDES me through the formative decades of my life. Through the complex relationships with a lot of baggage and bitterness that we both carried from our childhoods. Through becoming a mentor and a daddy anyone could have dreamt of for my little daughter, and through making and losing A LOT on the way, financially speaking. It was a bittersweet ride that lasted 19 years; looking back, we had no regrets.

I have no regrets, not a single one, because I love what it shaped me to be, and it is all because of our journey together. I have the highest understanding of the world through Les showing me what is out there. Food, drink, culture, travel, knowing what is "correct" for us and what is very "incorrect." We are both Split definitions by Human Design and found the other half in each other. However, this was not a perfect match by Human Design connection standards. He does not bridge my "gap". Our connection chart (theme 6-3, "better to be free") says we need to spend time apart for relationships to work. It is crucial to note here that someone bridging the gap in your Split definition does not mean they are the CORRECT person for you! And Les was correct for me to learn from, grow, mature and self-recognise.

And yet, he completed me.

I am saying it here as a tribute to my marriage and a stance. I hope you can also take a view like this. Being aware of our Human Design is incredibly empowering, but life does not happen "by the book". With all that awareness, we need to allow for the fact that it is not a rulebook or a dogma. It is about awareness and differentiation. It is about appreciating that everyone is different and allowing the differences to exist as we bond and build relationships.

Life will always have complications- even when the decisions are made correctly. We need mistakes and lessons to shape us into something more, where we can fully live out our potential. We do not need to seek perfection, even when it comes to Human Design and alignment in our businesses and marketing. At the end of the day, what is perfection but uniqueness? When there is nothing to compare to?

It is about making aware decisions so we can face the struggles worth facing and learn the lessons we are meant to learn to nurture our wisdom so we can later give back.

I think this is where the true beauty is, and I hope this book will give you the awareness to try, experiment, and even sometimes fail while fully understanding how it fits into the bigger picture of your life. For more guidance, do not hesitate to visit **marketingbyhumandesign.com**

# Part One

## Embracing Human Design

Chapter One

# A Beginner's Quest

## The Science of Differentiation

Human Design is a science of differentiation: it defines what makes you unique, what are your unique gifts, and how you can live out your true potential.

It was developed by Ra Uru Hu (born Alan (Robert) Krakower) from an experience he had involving a series of revelations from what he called the Voice in 1987. But he never claimed this to be his system. He referred to himself as a messenger to bring us awareness through this system, which is a specific combination of elements rooted in the ancient wisdom of I-Ching, The Book of Changes, and Astrology with a healthy mix of scientific flavour (biology, physics).

I love the story of this experience, as Ra joked that he barely knew his star sign when it happened, and he seriously suspected he was going insane at the start. The experience was so surreal. Yet after years of diving into the research, the Human Design System as we know it was developed and has been taught to his followers. It is now becoming increasingly popular worldwide as a system for uncovering your true potential and living a fulfilled life.

Oh, and let me mention that this system does not teach how to make money or run businesses. It is a self-discovery system and a guide for parents to bring their children up correctly according to their energy mapping and become aware of conditioning affecting us at every stage of our lives. So, no, there are no secrets in Human Design to becoming rich or successfully attracting clients.

The secret is to understand your true nature to leverage your natural resources, gifts, and potential for success - and choose what business and marketing strategies will feel more aligned.

Human Design is a complex system that doesn't have a "shallow end," so my goal here is not to overwhelm you with its history and complexity. I also have no intention to oversimplify it either, distort it in the process, or add to the noise surrounding Human Design as it becomes increasingly popular.

I merely intend to give you the bottom line of what it is about based on my personal research. I hope it will gently nudge you to experiment with just this information, watch, observe, and develop more TRUST in your life.

I want to encourage you to learn and experiment with trusting your Inner Guidance, loving and leaning more and more into your True Self, and learning the mechanics of your aura and how you interact with others energetically. In this way, you can choose more harmony and relax instead of feeling like a "hamster in a wheel" - which is pretty much how we are all conditioned to go through life by modern society.

In simple terms, Human Design is a map of how you are different, how your energetics operate, and a map to finding a flow in your life. I see a great use for this system as a compass to re-align your marketing strategies, find and unleash your Brand Voice within, and lean INTO your natural comfort zone. It does require stepping out of your conditioned comfort zone, which means letting go of some deeply rooted beliefs our parents and society have taught us for many generations...

*"Work hard!"*

*"Set goals and achieve them so you can BE Somebody!"*

*"Be better, be more!"*

*"If you want it, you have to 'earn' it!"*

*"Go get it!"*

Gosh, how exhausting!

Every day at 11:11 am, my alarm rings with a message: **SLOW DOWN TO ACCELERATE.**

Another synchronicity, as this alarm has been on my phone since 2014. However, it was only when I leaned into my Human Design experiment that I started truly noticing and understanding the magic of this statement. As I slowed down in my life, and especially in my business (which was terrifying), I discovered that, in fact, I am accelerating into the most empowering and fulfilling era of my entire life.

If you are a personality test junkie like me and are open to learning more about your energy and aura profiling, you will love Human Design. You will feel like you were just handed **permission to be you**, finally. Don't get me wrong — human life is full of lessons that don't always feel easy or enjoyable. But as they say, everything starts with awareness.

Think about it like operating systems. If you are running on Windows, applying keyboard shortcuts designed for a Mac won't work. It's the same for humans. Human Design makes you aware of your internal operating system. It gives you a manual for using correct shortcuts and understanding the processes underpinning the game's rules for your Design.

And yet, it is so much more than slapping on a label and telling you that there is this or that way you can operate. With the awareness of all the unique traits defined within, we can also learn about the magic of openness in areas without definition. We can discover how much wisdom and flow the understanding of this openness brings into our lives.

Business is such a personal thing, especially when you do it alone or have only a small team. When operating on a larger scale, the dynamics change, where individuality takes a backseat to collective efforts. But I assume you are a solopreneur, so this book is to show you that when we embody our Design and empower ourselves to show up in a way that feels good, it supercharges our business with the kind of spark that traditional strategies and tactics often fail to ignite.

If you are a complete beginner and have never done your Human Design chart, you will need an exact time and date of your birth, plus a place (nearest big city) to determine the correct time zone. I recommend getting your free chart generated at mybodygraph.com or geneticmatrix.com

Every second, you are penetrated by billions of the tiniest particles that carry energetic information (consciousness) from all large and small planetary bodies in our Solar System and beyond (in physics, they are called neutrinos). There are two major key moments in your life when your unique energetic map is created, and they are represented on the bodygraph.

In black, you see an exact consciousness imprint you received at birth when your body left your mother's body (your Personality, shown in black). Another imprint - at 88 degrees of where your Sun was before the moment of your birth - is an imprint that forms your subconsciousness (your Design, shown in red).

The chart has coloured-in parts that represent your definition: fixed, reliable themes/traits/energies that:

• Form your **Energy Type** (the way your aura is shaped and interacts with others in your world, hence giving you a specific Strategy for interaction to be in alignment with your Design).

• Give you reliable guidance on what is correct or not for you (**your Authority** for making decisions).

• Determine how you consciously perceive yourself and how others see you (the two lines in **your Profile**).

In a way, this is what you are "broadcasting" to the world: your unique energy map.

The chart also shows your openness (parts in white) that represent the experiences/themes/energies you are receptive to. This is where you take in conditioning from everyone and everything around you, including parents, friends, schools, society, religion, countries, and even our Solar System. This is also where you learn from these influences and gain wisdom around them, provided you know that this conditioning is not YOU.

The reality is that we are growing up, listening to, and taking in those outside forces without questioning. Eventually, we find ourselves identifying with them as who we are, ignoring the natural and authentic role we are given, and failing to find fulfilment in our lives. This is why Human Design was created for parents to understand better and guide their children to become who they truly are and to help them reach their true potential.

This is also why a lot of people get angry or do not identify with what they read in their Human Design reports. This is because they believe in their conditioning and believe that they are who they are not. Questioning that belief usually meets resistance, often severe.

This is why Human Design does not impose a certain rulebook on anyone's existence. This is why we call living your Design an experiment. As you start experimenting with listening to your Inner Guidance and following your Types Strategy, it soon reveals that many things you believe about yourself are simply not true. They only limit you from a much easier, joyful, and aligned life.

You truly do not need to know about every little detail of your chart. If you follow the strategy and Authority of your Human Design, you naturally unlock the gifts and start living out your potential. Or you can spend a lot of time digging into detail and still make decisions from your Mind and not out of your inner guidance. However, all this will eventually do is add more to your plate, burn you out, and leave you more confused about things that do not matter to you now. In this book, I will stick to the surface level to give you the compass, encouraging you to play with it in your daily life and your business and see what happens. It changed my life around. It turned my business into the channel for my self-expression of Truth (instead of a full-time job), attracted incredibly correct people to it, and boosted my profits without taking away my freedom - I would love you to experience this for yourself.

# Chapter Two

# You Are Your Brand

## Marketing is the aura of your business

It is how you attract your perfectly aligned clients and repel those who are misaligned. It is what makes your offers powerful and your messaging magnetic. It is what your clients rave about after working with you. Human Design takes second-guessing out of all these areas.

In this book, I am focusing on helping you let go of your fear of visibility and comparing yourself to others; find harmony with your True Unique self; start experimenting with it when making decisions and interacting with other people in your life; and confidently show up as the face of your business. Your business aura (your online visibility, the way you market yourself) is heavily based on your personal aura. **"People work with people."** This means that out of all your competitors, your potential clients are likely to choose you on the basis of whether they like you or not, and they will not invest with you (no matter if you are the best person for the job) if they dislike you.

And this is good news! Larger companies and corporations have to work so hard to develop their "brand identity," "mission statement," "value proposition," and all other made-up attributes, but YOU can lean into who you really are. Human Design gives you the manual for that operating system, the aura very specific in how you interact with other people and how they perceive you.

You no longer need to "come up" with your Brand. You ARE a Brand, a very powerful and very attractive brand. Irresistible to the CORRECT people for your gifts, offers, time, and energy. Your CORRECT people reward you financially and energetically for your guidance or service, creating transformations in their lives or businesses. It is that simple. The key is to stop inventing a brand you think they need or want and lean into what is naturally magnetic within you. I found that Human Design is the most accurate tool that points to your natural strengths and gives some practical suggestions.

Human Design also explains why you may have bought programs and coaching to teach you how to market yourself, and you applied everything as you were told, but it felt so off. Not only did it not bring the results you hoped for, but it also derailed you, disempowered you, and created a massive doubt if you are even cut out for all this.

I have been there, and not just once. I would see how the strategies worked for my coaches in action. I had proof that they were authentic and applied with integrity, but I felt like a fraud when I tried them.

At one point, I lost confidence in my abilities as an expert because I struggled to attract clients with those strategies. Somehow, I did better before I tried to "fix" myself, and then I just couldn't revert. I have been searching, trying, and testing so many strategies. I kept my business above the necessary line to meet my needs, but I still did not know or have a consistent way to attract aligned clients.

And then, I somehow discovered Human Design, and it felt like I received "**permission to be me**." At first, it took a little while to apply it all to my personal life, but soon my strategic left-sided brain started seeing how clearly this fits into running my business. Specifically, how I can market it, show up without feeling like I am begging for a sale with every post, and stop hustling and start living my Design as my unique True Self in business.

I started understanding how my personal aura affects my business aura. I even took it to the ninja level- determining what energy my business had based on the date when it became official and what energy this added to my magnetism. By the way, this may be a case of misusing Human Design, but I was just too curious and experimental.

Yet, at the end of the day, if you are a coach, consultant, or expert, it is you personally that people see, follow, and work with, and this is why I believe in focusing on your personal aura the most, especially in marketing.

# Chapter Three

# Human Design & Your Marketing Efforts

## Example: My Free Facebook Group Saga

In 2017, when I pivoted my business into visibility coaching after marketing other brands and businesses for almost two decades, it was as if I was beginning from scratch. Promoting yourself is a very different, personal thing. It does not matter how confidently I could create content and promotions for other businesses. When it came to promoting myself, it just did not feel the same. I felt utterly lost. I did not feel I knew what to do (despite so much marketing experience under my belt).

I already knew that I wanted to use Facebook as my centre stage. At the end of the day, Facebook was the platform that helped me with all my previous clients' promotions. I also knew that I did not want to use my business page, as by 2017, the visibility on the pages had become so limited. It was like sitting in an office all day, never leaving your desk, hoping someone would walk through the door. Not very effective when you really need to be seen to get more clients walking through that door in the first place. Trust me; Facebook Business pages may be great if you have an excellent validated offer to sell and you want to scale with ads. But if you do not have consistent business generated by a particular funnel without ads, if you are still figuring things out, a business page can be a very lonely and discouraging place to show up, no matter what you are telling yourself.

In addition to that, it is another way people try to "hide" from judgment out of fear of rejection. I am passionate about using our personal profiles on Facebook to connect, grow and nurture your audience as a coach or an expert, especially at the start (the first 3-7 years of your journey). And I believe that it allows for the self-empowerment required to succeed, as we are then faced with really evaluating our little fears, especially around judgments of others, and can see how unimportant those are in the grand scheme of your life's mission.

And NO - talking about your business, even about your offers, does not break any of Facebook's terms and conditions. The sales do not happen technically on Facebook. Anything that says otherwise has an agenda to scare you or force you to use pages, so they can sell you either ads or social media management. It is easy to add admins to the Business page, but logging into your personal profile is not something they can ask or take responsibility for, so they push the Pages agenda.

My issue is that they often sell it to clients who are not in any way ready for those kinds of services, just as I just mentioned, who are still figuring out stuff, which takes so much more than filling a 30-page client avatar workbook. In fact, it often takes years to figure out what works, and I wish more people spoke about how natural and essential this slow start is for your future success. Then when things are clear, you can change your strategy, tap into extended reach with ads, and hire social media management help.

But do not assume a social media manager will know what they are doing promoting your business if YOU do not know what you are doing in your business and marketing. That is what happens all the time, and this is why we often get stuck and frustrated. Because instead of figuring things out ourselves, we are looking for a magic wand that is just going to make everything work. And so many businesses out there will try to promise you that magic wand and sell it to you, even knowing you are the wrong persona for their kind of magic.

And it is also a fact that people will say anything when marketing their programs and services- whatever makes choosing their services the right thing for you. It is the nature of marketing, right? "Promise what they desire and convince them you are the best choice there is."

Think about a regular farmers market. The one that talks loudly about their tomatoes in the most attractive way gets the most sales. It is always all about personal magnetism and conviction with anything that can be sold to us.

Remember the tale about the Emperor's New Clothes? A merchant "sold" him nothing but described it as an exquisitely beautiful and quality fabric. The Emperor goes ahead because he is afraid to question the conviction that he is sold the "nothing", afraid to appear weak as he cannot see it, and then literally buys into thinking he is wearing the outfit. Everyone around him goes with the lie out of fear of offending him - except for one child.

I am that child right now. I want YOU to be that child as you are navigating the noisy world of marketing and business coaches, so you can find the way to see things as they are. Without thinking about what does not matter, without trying to give others the power to tell you what direction to go, you need to prove yourself.

Don't get me wrong. You can still speak with conviction and highlight what you help people with, their desires, and even their pain points, as long as what you offer is genuine after the transaction. There is potential for true transformation, growth, and authentic help. In this case, marketing your offers feels powerful. You KNOW you offer something truly special.

But too many times, the marketing of an attractive coaching program or an online offer just derails us from our path, as it truly speaks to what we would love to hear and believe, even if it is completely not what we need.

Do you see how with any advice, you need to be a little careful and always question the validity of it- both in general and related to YOU?

When you start experimenting with Human Design, this naturally happens. And to attract clients with your Facebook profile (and beyond), you just need to master the art of creating content that compels. This book can help you with many ideas on how to crank up your natural magnetism by talking from specific angles.

But then again, you will never know it if you do not try. Rant over. Back to my story.

I started using my personal profile and created content around what I could help people with, sharing my insights and my visions. Still, I felt I did not have the "secret key" to the successes being paraded by other coaches.

Just like everyone else who decides to start their coaching business, I fell victim to the "firehose" of marketing advice. One of the common strategies was to create a Facebook group where one can drive all those interested in the topic of your expertise to build connections and nurture members into buying one's offers and programs. It made perfect sense, and over the next two years, I built a group of over 1500 members.

Only to discover that **my free Facebook group never brought me any clients.**

It was more of a place where current and past clients who found me elsewhere came to hang out. But I already had a dedicated group for them elsewhere, so it felt exhausting to manage another free group only to see that nobody except current clients was engaging. No matter what I tried to build engagement in that free group - and I promise, I did everything "right" - it did not generate clients. It was like people joined for information and not to see if I was the one to offer them deeper levels of support and transformation. Only those who experienced my support firsthand were eagerly engaging with my content...

What a dilemma!

When I first thought of that, it did not even occur to me to look for the reason in my Design. I just assumed I was targeting the "wrong" people. So, I removed almost a thousand members who did not "fit my criteria" and started again targeting different demographics.

After a year, the group grew back to nearly 2000 members, but the outcomes did not change. Clients came to me through different channels, entered my programs, and then started engaging in the free group even more than the client group I built as an intimate hub for them.

This time I have been looking at my personal Human Design, and I knew that my 1/3 profile meant I am naturally introspective and self-absorbed - always focused within. People are not a crucial element in my immediate surroundings. I need people because I am a Projector (I will explain the mechanics further in the book), but my life journey is not about networking or even leading them anywhere. My journey is looking into something, processing it within, and sharing what I see.

People in my world get a massive value when I share my personal observations, perspectives, and insights of what I have been learning, researching, investigating, and seeing in others and then trying and testing (even though the testing part happens on a subconscious level.

I do not deliberately decide to "try" things, I go all in - and learn from my own mistakes of what does not work). That's a 1/3 profile trait in a nutshell.

I also learned that my mission has to do with a high sense of integrity. In other words, I have an internal BS barometer, which I sense immediately or quickly when something is out of alignment. (Conscious Mercury in Gate 18.3 helps here too) Line 3 makes it almost an obsession to re-align what I see, and this is where I have a great gift for various audits, especially to do with messaging (websites/content audits).

It helps me see clearly through the noise of the marketing industry, where most taught strategies just create more "busy-ness" and are either sold to people who are not yet ready for these strategies or they are not practical and effective to move the needle in your business more efficiently, unless a suggested strategy is perfect for your Design, of course!

This so obviously corresponded with my experience with running a Facebook group. Someone with my energetics simply does not need a place "to network." Neither do I need a place where anyone who is simply seeking a shortcut or a magic bullet to their struggles can join - without actually seeing ME as a guide first.

That is a crucial element for any Projector - we get to have a sense of true value to others only when we are with people who see and recognise our gifts (often a particular gift). Unfortunately, a free Facebook group was not such a place.

People could find it and join, not because of ME as a guide, but just to find answers to their questions. This created a very incorrect environment that then fed into my Projector's bitterness (feeling unfairly invisible) and forced me to start "working harder" to prove my worth to the group. Because that is what we, Projectors, tend to do when we are not surrounded by the correct people, it is ALL about the correct people – FOR US.

Let me clarify. This should not sound like a call not to show up unless everyone in your surrounding is a perfect match- whether you are a Projector or any other energy Type. Not at all. We need to show up and be visible in the most accessible places, so we can attract those correct people who see us and follow us for who we are.

But when it comes to your **inner circles**, that is where correctness becomes a deciding factor for Projectors, and even more so for 1/3s. Incorrectness is toxic. It penetrates all areas of our lives, literally robbing us of the life force energy and the desire to create and to show up.

I see my business as my inner circle; only the correct people are allowed in. No matter how much money someone wants to throw at me, if they are incorrect, it is a NO - a non-negotiable factor I learned the hard way throughout the decades in business.

What I needed to put all my energy into was SHARING my insights and my findings. Writing, blogging, podcasting (that is, up to this day, the only "networking" I do, as I enjoy both giving and hosting interviews and learning from my guests and hosts). Anywhere I could lean into my magnetism by Design as a 1/3 Projector.

Another area Human Design helped me see was that my gift is in one-on-one work because that is where my clients experience the most magic. Again, this is unlike all those loud gurus who advise us to "leverage" our time and go for group coaching as fast as possible. While I also enjoy a small group environment, the real transformation happens 1:1. That is a Projector's strength. I can leverage by raising my prices, but not at the expense of the impact I am here to make on each of my clients. Human Design ended up with years of confusion and made this decision an easy NOPE.

Do you know what is interesting? In a social scenario, I tend to lock on just one person at a time. I always find myself "lost" in a group, and it does not feel enjoyable for me unless I am talking to one person at a time, and we are going deep, too!

This awareness helped me avoid a lot of unpleasantries or even feeling ashamed because the awareness allows us to exercise kindness to those around us and ourselves. Otherwise, it is like getting upset that you have green eyes - there is nothing you can do about changing that fact. But you can own it and enhance it in whatever way you want. Whatever way makes you feel beautiful or powerful.

My Human Design shows zero need to NETWORK with strangers to attract clients. Strangers find me through the content I create, and THEN they come into my world - so they already see me as a guide.

I archived that Facebook group twice previous to this *A-ha!* moment, but there was always self-doubt that made me re-open it. So, the third time, I spent two days removing all group members one by one (which made my line 3 very happy - breaking bonds is one of its key themes). That was the end of a long struggle to have a free group as a part of my client attraction funnel.

Over a year later, I can confirm that it had zero negative effects, and my business has only boomed as I pour my creative juices into content and not try to "keep my group engaged," as the common Facebook Group Funnel strategy would recommend.

Now, on this topic, I have since created a group where I only allow people who have worked with me before, are my current clients, took one of my free trainings, or have read this book to join. In other words, you are allowed in if you have allowed me to guide you, to open a door into a new, more harmonious, and aligned way of showing up online. If you choose to take a step through it- you are welcome in my inner circle.

And it feels GREAT.

Chapter Four

# What Holds Us Back From Being Ourselves

## Cockroaches In Our Heads

I believe the biggest obstacles in our progress are simply our smallest but very persistent thoughts, just like the above example of having a group that you do not enjoy running and feeling "obliged" to show up there.

I call those thoughts "cockroaches in one's head" because they are disgusting and multiply and stop you from taking action. It is also a funny Russian saying I grew up with, and humour is a great way for me to cope with overwhelm. I hope you never had to live through an infestation of house cockroaches, but I can tell you firsthand - it is a terrifying experience that scars you for life! But it also taught me not to allow this to happen ever again – specifically in my mind.

I am a personality test junky. I am highly logical, a bit sceptical, practical, and strategic in my thinking. I tried applying so many different systems- Yung archetypes, Mayer-Briggs, Enneagram... whatever it is out there, I probably took a test for it. Some gave me some insights, even pretty inspiring ideas, but never the whole picture.

Human Design is the only system that I discovered that is so incredibly accurate in what POTENTIAL we hold, how to decondition ourselves from thoughts and beliefs that are not ours by nature, and how to use our design to build the life of our dreams. Our businesses are only a part of it.

Human Design is a relatively new concept, but it is gaining popularity, spreading like wildfire among people on the journey of self-discovery and realising their potential. Some refer to Human Design as a "user manual." Some say it is "permission to be you."

Human Design is not about getting a label stuck on your back: you are THIS, so you are like THAT. This is what happens with most personality profiling systems. For some people, it feels good and explains things they may have shamed themselves about. For others, it feels suffocating to be put in a box.

But Human Design is different. When you look past the initial labels, it basically says there is a Design, an imprint, an "operating system" that can remove the struggle if fully enabled. You get to lean into who you are, do things the way that is natural for YOU, and tap into the gifts and strength that you are born with while sampling and playing with your openness whilst interacting with the auras of others in your world.

This last part I love the most. We can learn what is ours and what is actually "borrowed." And like with everything borrowed, we can play with it, take pleasure in exploring it, and use it for what we want and need to do, and then return it and let go of it. It is not ours and does not need to create clutter in our lives.

Most people do not recognise that something they have does not belong to them. They cling to it, yet these beliefs, thoughts, and behaviours can only hurt them. Human Design's beauty is learning who you are and how you can "taste" or sample the energies that may not be "yours" without getting stuck in the long term. This is what "conditioning" means to me. When you learn about Human Design, a lot of conversation is around deconditioning. But, to me, that does not mean completely getting rid of something.

I fully admit that perhaps after another decade of experimenting with my design, I will have another definition of conditioning. That can happen. I have no idea what lies ahead or what way my perceptions, feelings, and understanding of anything will shape them. But for now, this feels very good.

For a couple of years, I went into some form of self-shaming for being "conditioned" this way or the other. I think it is the first reaction of everyone who comes to Human Design through the original creator's definitions. (The language used by Ra Uru Hu is not the most encouraging, but there was a valid reason for that, and this is a topic for another day.)

And then somebody said, "*Projectors are very vulnerable to conditioning*," and it clicked. I understood that doesn't mean that anyone with open centres is a victim of some evil brainwashing (this is how it feels at the start). It just means that we are flexible. We can literally penetrate the energy and aura of those with defined elements. We have a little taste or sample and use it strategically to our advantage rather than starting to believe this is IT for us.

I think this is particularly obvious in the marketing and business coaching industry. There could be a coach that you follow. You feel pulled and attracted to them. You secretly want to be like them. But their advice does not work for you simply because you do not see WHY not.

That coach could be a completely different type by design, and maybe they are here to trailblaze, create movements, and initiate things.

When you start following their strategies, you end up frustrated because you do everything they say, but somehow it doesn't feel right. When you brush that feeling aside, you get pushback from your audience or leads, and when you initiate, not much interest arises. You think something is wrong with YOU... But the only disadvantage is that you are trying to operate using another person's "operating system" manual.

It is like you are working on a MacBook but trying to use Windows keyboard shortcuts. They do nothing and make you feel frustrated.

Now, if you learn and master the shortcuts that work for YOU and YOUR operating system, everything falls into place and becomes a breeze.

And the other thing is that I know highly visible marketing and business coaches who are, for example, Manifesting Generators and have a lot of sacral energy. They move super-fast, can respond to their audiences, and initiate new projects quickly. They create whatever they want and fast, too. They then move to something else and still manage it all well.

You look at them, buy their programs, and try to implement them, but it feels so overwhelming and exhausting, and some strategies feel plain wrong. When you voice your concerns, these coaches look at you with slight disbelief in their eyes because it is so natural for them, so if you cannot do this, you must be making excuses or something... and you start thinking that maybe you are not cut out for it.

Well, I am here to tell you – you ARE!

You are just not seeing it. You are not focusing on YOUR brilliance and honouring YOUR energy levels and, most importantly, YOUR strategy.

In terms of what action to take, it could conflict with everything you have learned or tried. And yet it will work for YOU!

By the way, not every Manifesting Generator is set for success in marketing, and it doesn't mean that if you are a Generator, a Manifestor, a Projector, or a Reflector that there is no way you cannot be super visible and super successful while feeling really good about it. **It is about doing it YOUR way without trying to be someone else.**

Marketing and specifically online visibility by Human Design, is the niche I am focusing on in my business. I said so many times that I am not interested in becoming a traditional Human Design coach. I fully understand that a current "trend" is moving into Human Design, and that is ok.

What I am doing here, and I know this in every part of my body, is following my calling and not jumping on the bandwagon. In fact, most Human Design coaches who talk about business have never built any businesses except for their own. There are a few that had massive successes in it, financially speaking, and there are a few incredible experts that are naturally intuitive with their guidance. Yet most advice I come across is just repeating something generic. I am sorry to say that, and yet there is not enough industry experience as a business coach or marketing expert to discern between what is effective and what is more busy-ness, even though it may sound aligned to certain energetics. This is what makes me tick.

I spent so many years trying to discover why certain strategies are such nonsense. When you look at the foundational level and expose them, you find the same strategies presented and masked under Human Design "flavour". This feels appalling to me. This is where the question of integrity arises for me. This is where I urge you to use your inner guidance and your Authority to determine if something feels right for you, and NOT look at the shiny cover or personal success and charisma of the coach teaching you these strategies, EVEN if it is me.

By the way, when you read about Authorities, pay attention to how many times there is a warning about other people's chemistry affecting your decisions and clouding your inner guidance! Beware of that.

I was holding myself back for over a year and trying to deny that I wanted to position myself as a Marketing by Human Design expert before I actually "announced" it and started walking my talk. I really did not want to jump on the bandwagon, as Human Design has been spreading across the coaching industry like wildfire over the last couple of years.

I did not want to be a "woo-woo" coach, so I kept trying to develop programs that used more traditional marketing strategies I knew and implemented, even though I secretly hated my offers and couldn't get myself to promote them properly either. This was my cycle for a couple of years: I would create and fill a program and look after my clients very well inside it. However, when it came to launching it again, I just couldn't; I felt like there was zero motivation. What I was offering, the actual strategies, made full sense and even worked for some clients really well, but teaching them did not bring me the feeling of success I desired.

So, I doubted myself and tried to look for a solution on the outside. I thought, "*Maybe I am just bad at sales?*" So, I gave away my power to lead generation trainings and sales coaches, and I tried to follow them without even thinking if what they suggested I do was aligned with who I am. And yet nothing worked until I decided to look for the answers within and leaned into my personal Human Design experiment 100% in Business just as much as in my personal life.

I slowed down to a point where it felt REALLY scary. I stopped promoting anything- just holding onto current clients and the revenue that was generating. I stepped back completely, allowed myself to stop DOING, and focused on just BEING. I dived into what draws me:

studying, looking after myself on every possible level, and spending more time and money on a lot of self-care than I have ever allowed myself before. I discovered the joy of getting a professional facial treatment at 45. I put myself first and created an energetic space for opportunities.

And then it came... a big exciting, all-consuming wave of CLARITY. I suddenly understood what was ACTUALLY happening. All that time, I was sampling and testing (my line 3) and experiencing the conditioning that we should always ensure we deliver "results." And yet my zone of genius was not in delivering results to people or delivering any kind of doing-based service or solution. I was someone who ordered a new perspective, a breakthrough. I saw clearly that my genius was in "opening doors" to a new way of seeing things. And I felt so recognised and successful (my Projectors alignment feelings) every time I could "open a door" for a client. My coaching and mentoring are all about the PROCESS, the personal breakthroughs, a-ha's, and tiny but powerful shifts that some of my clients experience on EVERY call.

That is what I am here to be – a guide, a confidant, and an advisor. Not a DOER, or a builder, or a leader of a movement.

Finally, a full body KNOWING - Human Design was not just here for my personal transformation. It is a DOOR that I am here to open for others who are looking to create more harmony in their businesses. More joy, satisfaction, peace, more success through feeling good about making aligned choices and expressing themselves in the most natural and empowered way.

This is what I want to help you with – to discover how to market YOUR brilliance YOUR way. For more guidance, do not hesitate to visit **marketingbyhumandesign.com**

# Part Two

## Your Role In the World

Chapter Five

# How Deep is Deep Enough?

## Beware of "Seduction by Knowledge"

In this section, we are diving deeper into your Human Design Type. Each type has a specific aura and how it operates when interacting with others. It also has a particular Strategy to ensure the most harmony and alignment. This knowledge may change how you show up in business and life forever. It can help you avoid burnout by choosing the best way to spend your energy, along with activities that also aid with this. It gives you a very reliable way to decide on your offers in the most efficient and impactful way for your energetics and a go-to decision-making compass for any opportunities, ideas, and initiatives. With this awareness, you will know what to let go of, outsource, and delegate. You will understand your natural magnetism and lean into it in your Brand Identity and voice.

But first, I must ask you to have an open mind and heart. Forget what you think you "should" be or do. Try looking at this from a fresh perspective, especially if you are unfamiliar with Human Design. Or if you are familiar with it but haven't applied it to your marketing. After all, this could be the start of the rest of your life!

Another disclaimer, and this is not just my observation: when we come to Human Design, it is such a complex area that there is no "shallow end" in it. As we realise how accurate and empowering it is, we start getting pulled into the depth, wanting to know every meaning of every gate, channel, planet, etc. I would love to say to you, **STOP before you get overwhelmed.**

Ra Uru Hu, the original teacher of Human Design, stressed - almost in every training I have listened to - that knowing every detail is only essential to those who intend to become Human Design Chart Readers. What everyone else needs to master to find the alignment in their lives is simply their **Type's Strategy and their Decision-Making Authority.** Everything else clicks into place and activates only when you follow your Strategy and Authority.

I firmly believe that understanding your Human Design Profile Lines is paramount for marketing purposes. After all, they underpin your personal brand. So, you can consciously lean into the specifics of your Brand Voice. And yet again, it is only by following your Strategy and Authority that you can leverage that understanding by expressing yourself in the right place, at the right time, and in front of the correct people. It all depends on your top-level Design.

So, unless you have a substantial inner calling to become a Human Design professional, please trust me (and Ra Uru Hu) when we ask you to let go of constantly learning and start practising and, over time, mastering that most crucial part of your experiment. Your Strategy. Your Authority. Everything else will fall into place.

But of course, I will also talk about some more juicy details in this book to give you something extra to satisfy your thirst. Just keep in mind that I am also a student on my path to Mastery, so while I try to keep my information correct, this is not a textbook. It is what I researched, learned, and understand right now. I believe my level of understanding will deepen over the next few years, and I may produce the next version of this book. But for now, my findings are all you need to get started and SUCCEED. Because, as a Projector, I am here to inject you with success - and I am on a mission to do exactly that!

It had been an obsession for a few years before I officially decided to use Human Design in my business. Now it is a compass to help my clients build online visibility and market their business in a way that feels safe, enjoyable, empowering, and authentic to them and how they are designed to operate. That is precisely how I felt when I came across it in early 2020. It took over simply by reflecting on who I was so accurately: my struggles, insecurities, gifts, strengths, and potential.

Unlike a personality test that you may take while in a very "dark" or too "elated" place and get the results reflecting your emotional state at the time of the assessment, your Human Design is more an energetic imprint that defines specific fixed energies you are broadcasting to others. It also shows your receptors where you constantly receive such broadcasts from others, processing them, gathering wisdom and sending them back into the world amplified.

It is the science of energetics and how we interact through electro-magnetic forces in our auras. You may call it "vibes." Or perhaps you experienced being with someone and suddenly feel unexplainably sad or start thinking about things that are not important to you. This can happen when you have some openness picking up on other people's energetic transmissions that you then amplify in the form of emotions, thoughts, fears, and beliefs that do not belong to you.

Human Design traditionally divides humanity into four types: Generators (67%- including Manifesting Generators), Projectors (23%), Manifestors (9%), and Reflectors (1%).

Before continuing, I want to mention that Human Design is an incredibly accurate "navigation" system because it promotes the idea of differentiation and doesn't put anyone in a box. We are using a bunch of labels to identify specific energetics and traits. However, everyone is unique because there are so many other elements at play – just like in DNA- creating an extraordinary and unique energetic imprint that shows what themes are consistent for you and where there is room for expansion and gathering wisdom. Personal development and business have always been intrinsically connected, so I will boldly say that you can boost your business by experimenting with your Design.

# Chapter Six

# Generators & Manifesting Generators: Born To Know Themselves

## Create Joy & Relax Into the Flow

Our world is built by Generators, who make up over two-thirds of humanity (67%). It evolves, expands, and thrives because of those fabulous Generator types. Generators are the Creators of life itself. If you are a Generator type, **your business is truly HOW you are helping to shape this world.**

I see amazing Generators and Manifesting Generators in the online coaching world, always showing up and shining in their joy. If your Type is a Manifesting Generator - you are still a Generator at your core, so this section is for you too.

Generators - you have an open and enveloping aura. Your aura is like a mesmerising whirlpool that effortlessly pulls in the Universe around you, allowing you to pick up on its cues and respond with a special built-in navigation system right in the lower part of your torso: your Sacral Centre. You are constantly responding to what is presented to you - expanding with joy and light when it is correct and contracting when it is not correct.

How I wish your parents knew to teach you to watch that beautiful "dance" with the Universe that you are engaged with at every moment of your life. But the reality is that your mind is often so much louder (and so impatient to jump into action if you are a Manifesting Generator) that, unless you consciously start practising listening to those body responses, they are often left unnoticed entirely.

Let's park that for a second and go back to that wide, powerful, attracting aura of yours. The reason it is shaped like this, and it works in this way, is because it helps you **figure out the most important answer you are here to ask: WHO AM I?**

Yes, energetically speaking, you are here to focus on WHO YOU ARE and find the joy and satisfaction of being WHO YOU ARE. **It is not about "them" for you. It is all about YOU.**

Before you start jumping the gun, consider that this is not about selfishness. On the contrary- this is about tapping within to spread that joy and light into the world. It all happens through that aura of yours.

It is so easy to interact with. When I am with a Generator or a Manifesting Generator, I always feel like I am being hugged. Happy, aligned, deeply satisfied Generators are constantly pumping the Life Force energy through their aura into the outer world. This is what makes them so magnetic to the rest of us. And that is the key to accessing that Life Force energy within- whatever you are doing has to feel really joyful to YOU. It can only magnetise others when you love YOU in it (doing it, being it).

When it starts feeling like a chore, the light goes off, and with it goes the energy to get anything done. Generators can often feel stuck and frustrated when they keep pushing against that "wall." And when they are frustrated, they do not see WHO THEY ARE. There is just emptiness.

That is when some can start quitting or even struggle to start anything (a problem more significant for non-Manifesting Generators). The Manifesting Generators are designed to do so many things at once. They might be focusing on something else while procrastinating on others. Regular Generators can often be completely stuck in inaction! But when they love what they do, when they focus on activities that feel joyful and satisfying, they have incredible stamina to create and keep creating.

## Generator Strategy: Wait to Respond

You are here to **relax into the flow of YOUR lif**e. This is the hardest but the most rewarding mindset shift you will ever need.

When taking action, as a Generator, you are designed to respond to what life presents you. Every moment of the day, you are physically responding to what is happening in your Sacral Centre -specifically **outside your Mind or body.** Your aura is designed to pull in people, events, and actions so that you Sacral can Respond to them. All you have to do is wait to be "served" and follow your Sacral responses.

Waiting for it does not make you in any way less powerful. In fact, when you Respond with a "*Hell yeah!*" (expansion feeling inside) and follow your Authority (more on it further in the book), you can then take action with full force. You do not need to wait to respond to any small aspect of this action as long as you did not initiate it in the first place. When a Generator only takes action in response to those outside cues - they become a magnet for perfectly aligned opportunities and people appearing in their lives as if by sheer luck.

**Synchronicities are a great sign of living in alignment for a Generator.**

Generator, you are here to connect to YOURSELF, maintain and build conditions for even more life, joy, passion, love, family, and happiness. Your aura is focused on groups, contributions, collaborations, and togetherness. It is a perfect aura to have for building communities. You need people in your life to feel alive and respond to.

There is one little insight when it comes to having to wait. It is all about the availability of energy for a particular task. When your Sacral responds – you get to tap into the life force energy. If your response is negative – it indicates that you do not have the available energy for a specific task – right that minute. I recommend the Visibility By Design podcast episode I recorded with a Human Design Guide, Alannah Hillstrom, where she offers great advice and an explanation of the availability of Sacral energy. I think it sums up what Responding is in a nutshell. Your body has an in-build GPS that says, "Yep, have the energy for that" or "Nope, do not have the energy for this". And it can be illustrated not like an ON/OFF switch but more like a wave of expansion and contraction. In another example, you can Respond, feeling available and expansive, for example, to a conversation or a task, but as you are "in it", the wave can start going down. Sometimes it could make you doubt if you have made the right choice, but the secret is to give yourself a little rest, and then the energy comes back. Train people in your life to ask you if you are "available" or whatever they need from you. **You need a YES/NO question to feel the Response.** If it is a no, ask them to check in with you in a while or that you may do it at another time.

A tip for tapping into the Response when no one is around is simply to make a list of tasks/opportunities and ideas and ask yourself, looking at each of the listed entries, "*Do I have the energy available for it right now?*" If not, do not feel back transferring it to another time. How simple? How wonderful – you can get so much more done this way without overthinking!

## Common Blocks: Overcoming the Grip of 'Shoulds' and Perfectionism

Remember that through this open aura, Generators are likely to be the most conditioned Type. Following gurus and focusing on "shoulds" rather than their desires is a massive and widespread issue. Putting themselves and their needs last and doing tasks they do not enjoy just because they believe this is "how it's done." In this conditioning, Generators can be quite stubborn and even pretty reactive in the lower energy spectrums. They keep pushing and pushing, often trying hard to be high achievers. And when they do not get the same reciprocated energy back, they can feel very let down and even victimised.

Can you see how everything turns sour when a Generator doesn't focus on figuring out WHO THEY ARE and instead tries to figure out others in their world? The Generator's energetic blueprint is not designed to focus on others but on themselves. Follow the blueprint, and you will see how magically you start attracting the correct people into your life the more you focus within, not in a selfish way, but through self-discovery and self-realisation.

It is not about shoulds. The "Should" mindset comes from homogenisation - which means trying to make everyone the same. But we are all so different. You are so unique in your BEING, in who you are... shoulds are only taking you further from your true authentic self-expression.

In marketing, this can look like trying to follow someone else's processes, spending time and energy on tasks that your sacral is responding all the time negatively, only because you think you "should" be doing them (or because that charismatic coach you invested with tells you to). And on top of that, you are overpreparing, trying to be perfect, forgetting that any big shiny authoritative figure out there started from nothing, as imperfectly as they could and did not have everything so polished and smooth, yet they made it where they are right now over TIME.

Tony Robbins slept in the back of his car when he started working. I waitressed tables and managed restaurants for over a decade when I moved to Ireland. You do what you have to do to start. Then you can focus on positioning yourself, but only just above where you are, so it does not overwhelm you and rob you of your joy.

I personally believe that **focusing on a stage way too far ahead is the biggest problem for Generators**, who need to focus on one step at a time, mastering it before moving to the next one. Even without any Human Design reference, the worst thing one can do is to think too far ahead - this makes us skip important foundations that construct a secure solid base for everything we build in our businesses. Understanding what "stage" your business is at right now is the most crucial awareness, so you can choose to focus on what matters right now and create stability and sustainability where you are. Then you will focus on the next step.

Of course, programs like "100K in 90 days" do not help you think clearly at all, playing on your excitement and willingness to skip steps. It is not your fault. Every adult forgets how long it took them to learn how to walk. We expect things to be fast and easy. But it is not how life or building a business works.

Another issue I see is expecting results sooner than they often tend to happen. You see, Generators have a much slower pace of how things happen in general. Manifesting Generators are lucky as they can get lots more done at the same time, but then they skip important steps and have to go back to fixing things...

Comparing yourself to those who seem to "get there" faster can be discouraging at best. Yet, trusting your pace and your journey is key because staying in your lane allows you to focus on mastering each step or skill at hand. So, you get there slower but steadier and with a solid foundation and mastery of every previous step. **The only person you can compare yourself to is YOU yesterday.**

## Embracing Plateaus As Fuel for Generator Brilliance

And this brings me to a natural trajectory to success for a regular Generator. It is not a steady diagonal upward rising line. Not even a zigzag. Your trajectory looks like a staircase. You master that one skill or step, and then you hit a period where things start becoming a little unclear, a plateau. Sometimes it comes with a bit of frustration. This is good news!

It is a checking-in moment for you. It can indicate that the break-through is ahead; you have "completed your level" and waiting for the new one to load. Or maybe you are waiting to fight the levels' "boss." It is literally like a video game progression for you.

Sometimes the plateau also gives you a chance to check in with yourself - are you still following what lights you up? Did you add or focus on something because you felt you SHOULD, not because it was very enjoyable for you to be busy with? Talk to someone you trust that can ask you yes/no questions about what you do. And then, follow your sacral responses to decide what to keep and what needs to change. Or if you are trying to "walk through the wall," when all you need is to turn left or right...

Plateaus are good for you. This is the natural way things evolve in your life, and leaning into these mechanics will help you let go of frustration and honour, staying in your own lane and taking time to get to your destination. You are not in any way "worse" than any other type, and the bottom line is not even about when the results are coming but how you feel right now!

**Focus on figuring out whether you are adding to WHO you are**.

If yes, focus on **feeling the satisfaction** from what you are doing (or find what you feel satisfied doing) and let the rest - clients, money, opportunities - come to you. That feeling within pulls them in. This is your magnetism in action.

If it doesn't add to WHO you are, perhaps it needs adjusting or even taking off your plate. Trust me; you can get business success with a very minimalistic setup if that is what works for you. We tend to do so many things that do not bring many results (the classic 80/20 principle - the 80% of your results come from 20% of the effort you are putting into it.) Figure out what that 20% is in your setup - and let go of the rest for now.

Manifesting Generators are still Generators, as I mentioned, in the sense that this is about figuring out WHO THEY ARE and tapping into that feeling of satisfaction from being who they are - but their pace is completely different.

It is vibrantly unpredictable and multidimensional; so many things are happening at the same time. And you ARE designed to handle many things at the same time. The only secret is to **follow your passion**. When it switches off mid-task, just leave what you are doing for a bit - try focusing on something else that you love doing. Get back to this task when you feel you want to do it again (and you will when you experiment with switching between tasks).

The biggest issue I am observing with Manifesting Generators is **PUSHING**. Something does not work out, and they start pushing with an enormous force. And all they get back is the same massive force but in the form of **resistance**. Yet, if only they step back from the problem, go do something they actually love doing (and rebalance themselves energetically by focusing on the joy) - the solution to their problem will arrive smoothly and with the best possible outcome.

And, of course, all this will require relaxing into the NOW for you, which is the most important element of **the Generator strategy**. Not initiating, not being a go-getter, but relaxing and allowing the Universe to bring opportunities and signs for where to take action TO YOU. You are the vortex. You pull in the right people, opportunities, and energies, but only when you focus on the light within - YOU!

## Mind vs. Responding - Show Your Mind the Proof

Here is the thing, as a Generator, when you start following your strategy to respond, you will start understanding that you are here to simply SURRENDER.

But before you can do that, before you can master responding as your strategy and specifically take inspired action in response, you must understand that it starts with a mental process. This is why it is so hard when you learn about your Human Design strategy, and it says that you have to do something completely "illogical" and against what we are conditioned to believe. And this is why you have to work WITH your Mind, not against it. This is where you need to seduce your Mind to be on your side in this process. You have to get it to do what it loves best - research.

The Mind is deeply resistant to the Generator waking up. It always holds onto the Not-Self strategies as its way of maintaining control over you. Not-Self is not something bad. It is just exactly what the name says, not YOU, energetically speaking - it is what you pick up and believe to be through conditioning.

Your Mind will question everything it is presented with. The Sacral response for a Generator is a response to what is TRUTH for you. If presented with something very aligned and correct, it lights up, flowing through your body like bubbles or butterflies. Different people describe the feeling differently, but the general consensus is that this is a physical experience of something flowing through your body from under your diagram outwards.

Ra Uru Hu described the Sacral as "*like a motor that's never been used properly, and the moment you begin to use that motor properly, that is the moment that you begin to literally give it authority, slowly it begins to gain that authoritative power.*"

But your Mind will always fight this process, and here is why. When you start making your decisions in response, you are literally starting to live according to the NOW (there is a little extra patience required when you have an Emotional Authority before you take action, but it is still all about responding in that one moment). It is so essential you start living in the NOW, and this is very scary for your Mind. Sooner or later, you will hit that wall of fear of the unknown ahead because there is nothing for your Mind to build dreams and goals, and targets towards anymore. And it starts freaking out and literally finding any reason to "talk you out of" following your strategy, any evidence to prove how ridiculous it is...

And yet the true SURRENDER moment happens when you can respond and trust your inner guidance and your TRUTH without knowing what is going to happen and without being afraid of it. You are secure in your Design, your Strategy, and your Authority.

This is not something that can happen overnight, not at all. But you can start changing the way your Mind thinks by practising responding and trusting your Authority and then allowing your Mind to start believing this is working by documenting and analysing what happens when you listen to your Sacral, to your gut. And catching yourself when the Mind takes over in fear. Bring it back to trusting your journey. When it comes down to it, you are the energy type that has direct guidance and support for Life itself around you.

This presents us with a lot of difficulties when it comes to marketing. It is all about planning and hitting goals and targets in business. But I am not suggesting that you do not plan. All I am saying here is that when you are creating offers, use your strategy to respond. If you are planning a launch and you see or hear something and your body responds negatively, listen to it - make tweaks, reassess if there is something you are adding to your plate that feels suffocating, and perhaps you can simplify your process by focusing more on tasks you enjoy.

There is a danger with Human Design to see it as Dogma and start holding back at every step, questioning if you are indeed Responding or Initiating. Remember, this is your Mind tricking you into doubting yourself. The more you practice responding (start with everyday small things), the more you build the inner trust that you are guided towards (or away from) YOUR TRUTH.

At the end of the day, living your Design is an ongoing experiment where what you do is build awareness and figure out what is correct and what is incorrect FOR YOU. Uniquely. It is not a set of strict rules to live by.

## Decoding the Energy Equation: The Difference between Generators & Manifesting Generators

Now let's talk about the difference between Manifesting Generators and regular Generators. Some Human Design coaches separate these two Types completely, but then, there is so much misinterpretation out there, trying to popularise Human Design (and succeeding, I must mention). I prefer going to the source - the original interpretation by the creator of the system himself. At the end of the day, the Generator's strategy is to respond to the life on the outside. Everything I have written above applies to Manifesting Generators just as much, and it is even more difficult for them because, on top of the trickster Mind, they have to deal with their worst enemy - impatience.

One of the great approaches for Manifesting Generators to keep their Mind a little happier is visualisation. If they have an idea, they can visualise it, and then they can wait to see if a sign comes in from the outside supporting the idea - BEFORE they take action on implementing it.

This is the key to initiating before responding. There is a crucial element that will be missing - Universal support- so the task can end up meeting a lot of resistance, frustration, and overwhelm. Whereas when there is a little nod from the Universe confirming the "green light," you can experience a much smoother journey with lots of positive synchronicities and serendipity along the way.

Both Generators and Manifesting Generators are here to discover their **Rhythm of Life** - but where these two subtypes differ is the nature of the rhythm.

Regular Generators need to focus on one thing/one process at a time. Mastering each step before moving to the next step. And judging their progress by how much resistance they are meeting. If there is resistance- it is a great sign to stop and reassess if they are adding tasks that are not adding to their joy. Perhaps because they think it should be done OR, what is worse, they are doing it to "meet others' needs."

Manifesting Generators can handle multiple tasks simultaneously. Their rhythm is following what they want to do in that moment and allowing themselves to switch between the tasks if what they are doing suddenly loses its charm in the moment. Such a simple but powerful solution to feeling great about things they do.

Of course, this presents the challenge of having too many ideas and not knowing what to focus on next, losing inspiration mid-way and forcing yourself to finish, or feeling like you can never finish what you started. There is also the challenge of not knowing how to package your multifaceted personality into something clear and comprehensive to "sell." And, of course, not having the patience to "wait to respond" when you feel so lit up and inspired to take action.

Before I move on to the next type, I want to discuss the **Multi-passionate.** Very often, I see that word describing Manifesting Generators, and yet, regular Generators can be just as multi-passionate. It feels like there is a dissonance in the Human Design information out there.

I met several Generators who were pretty upset about this and wondering how come they are so multi-passionate, and nobody in Human Design mentions that. My understanding here is that most people, regardless of their Human Design Type, are multi-passionate, whether they consciously like calling themselves that or not. But with Manifesting Generators, because of **the pace** I DESCRIBED, the passions can all co-exist and be actively involved in - pretty much at the same time. Do something you love, half an hour here, an hour there, 5 minutes here, and it seems like so much is going on - we are so multi-passionate!

But those who are not Manifesting Generators by Design can have just as many passions. They just only have the capacity to focus on fewer things at the same time - and it is not a negative thing. A slower, one-at-a-time thing approach works in harmony with their natural energy pace and how they get to experience life, breakthroughs, and find safety, security, and purpose in their lives. Everyone is uniquely different, and whatever way each of us is designed is perfect for experiencing this lifetime in the best possible way. Learn the lessons you are here to learn and fulfil the destiny you are here to fulfil. It is the perfect design to reach your full potential. This is why trusting it pays off so well.

## Visibility For Generator Types

The biggest mistake you can make as a Generator is to focus on the outside - what you should be doing, how to be perfect or do something perfectly, on being "ready". And yet all your answers are inside, and you are equipped with a continuous response mechanism to tell you what is right and what is wrong for you to do or try in your visibility.

When you follow the "shoulds", you have no access to the life force you need to succeed, meet resistance in the form of frustration, and you will want to quit. Or you won't start in the first place.

Please, please try to be more "selfish" in your marketing. If your existential question is WHO you are, this is also the question that should drive your online visibility. Show them WHO you are - not in your direct area of expertise, but as a person. I am not talking about sharing any private details that you do not want to share. But there are passions that light you up, and people can connect to you through those passions (when you are lit up and magnetically pulling them in with your aura) - and then, as a way to have more access to you, they can pay more attention to what you do through your business.

What happens with many Generators I meet is that they separate themselves from their business, and so the business does not have their natural passionate essence in it. Trust me, as a very private person in my personal life - you cannot do that. You ARE your business. Business is one of the ways you express yourself. The more connected you show up, the more people will come to your light and give you an opportunity to respond and create something that will bring fulfilment as well as material benefits to you and the transformation you offer to your clients.

There is no "right" or "wrong" way for you to show up. It will be correct for YOU if you "do you" at all times. Lead with the elements, tactics and ways to express yourself that light your fire and give yourself permission to ignore the rest of the suggested tasks, especially if they frustrate you.

One more thing, stop people-pleasing. Stop saying yes to opportunities or commitments that do not light you up! You will appreciate how much space this can create in your life and business and unlock creativity for creating in your marketing. For more guidance, do not hesitate to visit **marketingbyhumandesign.com**

# Chapter Seven

# Manifestors: Born To Impact

## Just let Them Know It's Coming

Manifestors, I truly love you... You are not designed to be available to everyone, and you are not designed to be dependent on anyone in any sort of way. Embracing your internal compass requires the act of repelling others—a necessary step- and your aura takes care of that (akin to your energetic immune system).

Manifestor, you are the only Energy Type in Human Design that is essentially in control of your own destiny. How cool is that? Well, of course, in order to live out this potential, you need to understand the energy mechanics and your typical type of conditioning, so you can lead yourself (and others) in an empowered way.

Manifestor is a pure Energy Type. If you look at your bodygraph, there is a defined channel coming to your Throat from a motor centre. The motors in our bodygraph are Will (Heart), Solar Plexus (Emotional), and Root. The channel can be connected to the motor directly (from Will or Solar Plexus Centres) or indirectly (from the Root via the Spleen Centre) - making you a Manifestor.

See how the energy is flowing from those motors right into the Throat Centre? The Throat in Human Design is all about Manifestation, Action, and Expression. The energy in your design is being expressed through the action of initiating or igniting some form of IMPACT. What it is specifically is discussed further in this chapter.

One thing to remember is that as a Manifestor, you do not have the Sacral Centre defined, which means there is no consistent access to available life force energy. Your energy will come in waves and pulses, depending on where it is rising from. You will need periods of recharging and inaction in order to gather the momentum for initiating that action, which can sometimes take much longer than you would wish it did. You are not designed to hustle or try to do everything on your own. Learning to trust your energy patterns and creating the work and lifestyle around it is crucial for you to avoid burnout.

## Your Aura Is Your Armour

We have to talk about your aura because this is where a lot of misunderstanding and potential conflict resides in your interaction with people. Think about it- making an impact requires flexibility and freedom, so your aura is designed not to get "caught up" with others. It is small (literally very close to your body), and it is designed to be dense and is often called "repelling". This happens as you can often unintentionally give others a sense of unease around you, especially when you are initiating without warning.

But do not get hooked on it. There is a strategy for you to ease this tension: just remember that this aura is designed this way to protect you. It gives you independence from the influences of others to move fast and make the impact you are here to make - one initiation after another, without anything or anyone holding you back or trying to control you.

Let's look at the aura mechanics - your aura is very dense, and it resists penetration. In fact, when approaching a Manifestor, an aura of the other person will contract. Naturally, this can cause a sense of suspicion and unease. This is why your aura is called 'repelling," – but in reality, I have the most magical experiences with Manifestors I guide and know.

People put all sorts of labels to explain why they feel weird around you, so do not take it personally. It is natural that if someone feels they cannot approach you, they will start tiptoeing around you, not communicating openly with you, not getting to the point, or not keeping you in the loop. This in turn can make you feel impatient with them and angry (that can show itself outwardly or build deep inside). Anger is your red flag of being off track, of incorrectness and misalignment.

Keep in mind one very important thing - you are a Manifestor. You are not here to "be" with or do anything for others.

You have that lone-wolf energy. You do not need others to initiate unless they are correct for you. Your aura repels people who are incorrect for you for a reason. It saves you the resources and energy you need to make the impact you are here to make. It is your armour against the nonsense of others!

When you understand the nature of your aura, you can shift your perspective on what happens when you interact with people, as well as appreciate how it helps you have the space and freedom you need for doing what you want to do in peace.

## Making an Impact Explained

Let's talk about "making an impact" and what it means. This will vary, depending on your design, and it can even be confusing to some Manifestors. So, I want to start by putting you at ease: making an impact is not always about starting revolutions.

Sometimes it is all about starting a new way of thinking, starting a new trend, or starting a new perspective as you research something others have not gone into before. This is what initiating is all about. It is about what YOU creatively sparkle with, and it will, by your sheer nature, have an impact on the world around you. Big or small - but still an impact, nonetheless.

Think about that split moment when you light a match and fire ignites. It starts something new and powerful, something that can then affect and be used in so many life-changing ways. That fire is at the core of our survival as humans. It is extremely influential. And this is all about that energy that leads to Manifestor's purpose: it is to understand their impact on others.

**Your existential question is, HOW DO I IMPACT OTHERS?** This is where your wisdom comes into place. Manifestors are here to start, ignite, initiate, and trailblaze in whatever way they feel called to.

Interestingly, as I mentioned, most Manifestors are not consciously aware of how impactful they are (or can be). And often, they are quite challenging as children. Just to retain some form of control, their parents often express it in a way that makes little Manifestors feel that they should hold back in order to be loved: hold back their voices and their action.

Later, as adults, they can feel real anger when they are being controlled by others or by the conditioning they picked up within -

holding themselves back from impacting others. This feeling of anger is a red flag of living incorrectly, not understanding and honouring your truth and your role in this world. There is nothing wrong with anger itself- it is part of your design and its expression, but it is a compass for your decision-making. When you feel that anger, you need to check back with your Strategy and Authority to see what is misaligned and how it can be corrected.

You have everything required in your design, the repelling aura, with the energy flowing directly to the throat, to help you initiate anything that creatively boils within into the world. To birth the world.

You ARE the Big Bang.

## The Business of Informing

Just for a moment, as I know you like doing things solo, please hold my hand and let me give you a tour of this rabbit hole I explored intensively. I have done so much research, reading through hundreds of Instagram posts and blogs written by Manifestors to really get to the bottom of this Strategy to INFORM. Because the initial reaction of absolutely every Manifestor I know when they hear it is expressed in three simple letters...WTF.

And it is crucial to find a good explanation. First of all, informing is not about telling others what to do - this is just bossing them around, which will cause even more resistance and pushback. Neither is it asking for permission.

The Strategy for eliminating the resistance, creating the space you need to "do your thing," and at the same time allowing better communication with others in your life is simple. I think when you truly understand what it means and what following your Strategy allows you to achieve, you will love it.

The secret to finding that peace is about INFORMING those involved before initiating (literally just telling them what you are about to do) as well as something that does not often pointed out in Human design Instagram posts: **informing others how they can inform you!**

Let me repeat- it is **not about asking permission** to do anything. It is about letting people walking on the tracks know the train is coming. Your initiation is fast (like a train), and you are merely giving those who may be "walking on or near the tracks" on your way heads up to be prepared.

When you understand how your Aura is designed and learn to appreciate the freedom and flexibility it gives you, you become "kinder" to those who have to deal with this design on the outside. You know this Aura tends to make people feel uneasy, so you can focus on becoming a better communicator about how they can approach and inform you. Inform those around you before you start. Inform them of how they can keep you updated, how they can contact you, and what your preferred way to do this or that. In this way, they have a clear channel where they can keep you in the loop while you have "peace and quiet" to do what you want to do and make an impact in **PEACE - your signature feeling of alignment.**

All this density in your Aura is specifically designed to assist you in doing whatever it is you feel the urge to do. You do not need to "connect" to others in order to ignite, initiate and create something new and wonderful (for yourself or others). The only thing you need to master is your Strategy for removing the resistance, and it is all about INFORMING. Have I said it enough to sink in? I believe in repetition as the way to really nail something down.

Informing is literally saying what you are doing before you are doing it - as a statement. And to clarify - this does not apply to creating content or putting out offers on your Facebook page or your website. Your Strategy is only to make sure that you are informing anyone directly involved in what you are doing, and this does not mean your wider audience. Go create whatever you desire; this is what you are designed to do!

For example, if you and I were having a business meeting and you suddenly remembered you have something for me in your bag in the office - if you just get up and go (like many Manifestors sometimes do), it will leave me stunned and baffled. It would be me thinking, WTF and experiencing the "50 shades of black" of not-so-pleasant emotions towards you.

But if you just said anything like, *"I have something, one sec!"* Then my rainbow can truly shine all its bright colours, and I am excited to see what you have in store for me! Do you see the difference?

Simple statements of what is happening, like-

*"I am leaving", "I am doing XYZ", "I am getting something for you."*

This is where the magic is. You do not 'need' anyone to follow what you are doing. But **your Strategy is not about you. It is about them.** Softening the blow, in a way. By peacefully informing others, you can avoid the unpleasant confusion and resentment others may feel when they do not expect Manifestor's move.

And this brings me to Manifestors' signature feeling - PEACE. When you feel at peace, you are opening up more space for your creative sparkles - ideas, inspirations, and new projects. When you feel anger (which can also be a very suppressed passive-aggressive attitude) - it is a red flag that you have not followed your Strategy and are dealing with resistance.

I suggest an experiment for the next two weeks- try to inform those near you or directly involved about everything you do. Of course, you do not need to go out of your way and ring your sister to inform her you have decided to go shopping or watch a movie. But if you decide to go on holiday, you should at least in the passing mention your intention to anyone who might take you not telling them as a personal insult. (You know, people, they tend to do that!)

## The Power of the VOICE

We have to talk about your VOICE - because so often, Manifestors are brought up in a way that teaches them to keep their opinions to themselves, not to speak up, and generally disempowered in their manifestation skills. And yet the energy of ignition is hidden literally in their voices.

Let's look at Human Design energy flow. All energies in our chart - our energetic body - wants to be manifested, which means acted upon. However, the only centre that is an Action-taking centre is our Throat - the manifestation centre. And so, through the voice, the energies get to take physical form - in the form of action.

My biggest a-ha was realising that Manifestors in my life immediately and profoundly affect me. By just hearing them speak, I tend to suddenly fully mobilise myself and get into action on whatever was happening in my life at the time. I discovered it accidentally when after a week of procrastination, I had a very productive day, and when

I crossed off the last item on my list, I suddenly had an epiphany about why I was so on fire that day...

A Manifestor client sent me a bunch of voice notes on Messenger out of the blue that morning. Before I listened, I felt sluggish and demotivated, but after, I felt full of intention as if someone just started my engine. The voice notes were very personal; she was just letting me know about her holidays, so there was nothing logical about it, but after that day, I started paying attention. Every time I spoke or listened to a Manifestor, I felt ignited into doing what I needed to do. I even developed a playlist of my favourite Manifestors on YouTube that I started listening to on the slower days to get me started. Miraculously it works every time.

Naturally, it is not just about speaking. On a group call, if a Manifestor does not inform that they want to add something before they actually do it, it feels very heavy, like they are taking over the call. So here is an example of the power of just starting with-

*"May I add something?", "I have an idea you may like.", "I have an observation to share."*

Notice that these are not questions. They are not asking us for permission to speak. But they are so powerful, removing the uneasy feeling and actually enjoying the enthusiasm.

And so, let's think about the power of the voice. **It is not what you say. It is about you saying it!** Read this again.

As long as you are speaking out loud (on a video, on a podcast, on a voice note) - your magic works. So instead of fixating on WHAT you are saying, **start allowing yourself actually to speak and be heard.** It is not the exact words you use; it is how impactful hearing you speak is! Leverage this advantage when choosing your marketing tactics, and make sure you have videos whenever people need to take action - like just over your "Sign Up Now" buttons on your website.

When I create Marketing Blueprint By Design™ report for my clients, we focus on creating content types and choosing platforms that can help this magic spread. But I am honestly occasionally jealous of this superpower! You are also the only type that can initiate. So, any type of outreach- reaching out and asking more influential people for opportunities or connecting to others via Messenger for example- those are the strategies that you are energetically designed for. (Whether you have to do it if that does not make you feel inspired is a different story. You should only do what sets your creative juices on fire anyway).

## Breaking the Completion Norm: Manifestor Freedom

The last area I want to highlight is the need to FINISH what you started. Or should I say NOT FINISH?

Remember the match? Your purpose is NOT to be the match or fire burning it. **You are the moment of ignition**, and that is where your role ends. Anything that requires following through is not for you. It will burn you out and drag you into sometimes a very long-term period of apathy and exhaustion.

This is why you would do best in a lone-wolf scenario, where you either have a team (preferably Generators) who will feel so satisfied with the process of building your idea into something tangible or create a business that allows you to be that ignition. This can be an expert advisor, consultant, strategist, or someone hired to create something new but not expected to DO it all. This is exactly where you can choose how to run the business aligned with your energy type - there is nothing you "have to" do if it does not support your role.

Just let go of the idea of having to finish everything you started and the guilt that comes from quitting processes or not doing it all yourself. When you do, you will discover so much PEACE from knowing that you have the freedom to do whatever you want and freedom for your creative expression. If you think about your Voice - think about who may naturally need some ignition. Maybe this is something that will help you identify who to focus on in your business.

But again - who am I to tell you, a Manifestor, what to do?

Follow your inspiration. For more guidance, do not hesitate to visit **marketingbyhumandesign.com**

Chapter Eight

# Projectors: Here To Recognize

## Turn Your Light ON

As we delve into the world of Projectors, it is important first to understand the unique and energetic design that sets them apart from other Human Design types.

To start with, Projectors are not here to impact like Manifestors or master self-discovery like Generators. Instead, they have been designed with an innate ability to see the potential in others, and therefore they make excellent advisors and guides with a contagious sense for success. When we are correct, we simply inject everyone around and everything we touch with more success. How cool is that?

I am a Projector, and this might mean to you that I am an expert on this topic. I am NOT. Well, not on who I am as a Projector, for sure.

Here is **an important "thing" about Projectors - we are NOT here to figure out who we are**. In our energetic blueprint, our programming and the role of this specific design is to focus not on ourselves but on the other in our aura! Specifically, one person at a time.

A Projector is here to answer one question: **WHO IS THE OTHER?** And through the eyes of the other, perhaps get an idea of who they are, but truly, I often feel like it is all about **who we are when we**

**are WITH the other, in RELATION TO the other.**

When we try to figure out who we are, it just leads to complete confusion.

My daughter is a Mental Projector. She is only in her early 20s as I write this book, so it is all about figuring out who she is and "what to do to find joy" - as if she were a Generator. And the amount of anxiety and stress it causes her, almost on a daily basis, is quite upsetting. She is not consciously interested in other people (or so she believes) - but I see so clearly how she thrives when she is connecting to one of her friends or how stressed she is when she is worried about what an important professor might "think of her and her work."

There is much more than an energy type at play here, but the bottom line is that she is always completely exhausted - in my opinion, because her focus is not aligned with her energetic make. The more she tries to focus within - the more anxious and physically tense she becomes, and the more bitter she becomes about everything.

I am sure it is all part of the process for her, so unless she invites me to guide her, I am not welcome with my Human Design perspectives... I mentioned earlier that my daughter is working on her PhD in Theoretical Physics, and even a mention of a scientific explanation of Human Design, specifically the part about neutrinos, which I have no desire to bore you with in this book, ignites rolling her eyes so far, I often worry they get stuck that way.

I am saying all of this without a hint of bitterness because I clearly understand how the aura interaction works and how vital it is for me to be invited into guiding her (or anyone else).

## Projectors Aura

The Projector's aura is strong, laser-focused, and absorbing. It shines a strong beam on the other; it penetrates into the other's aura and allows the Projector to "see" and absorb their conditioning - in a perfect scenario, often resulting in asking the right questions or simply sharing something relevant that has the profound impact on the other person's direction. This makes Projectors such brilliant guides.

Projectors "see" into others, no matter if they agree to it or not; it is just how we are built, energetically speaking. However, you can imagine the pushback that happens if someone is not ready or interested to hear what we see. Unless a Projector understands why their advice/opinion/insight is "rejected," this can be a very painful experience. Depending on how bitter a Projector is already, it can range from feeling unfairly treated to full-on resentment, and in the case of some Energy Projectors, this bitterness can resemble Manifestor's rage.

This is why in personal interactions, it is crucial to hold back sharing what you see and wait to be invited, quite literally, into the role of a guide. Then these insights can be transformational for the recipient.

This is the crucial point to understand - how the Projector's aura interacts with other auras. It is the secret to how our content is consumed online too! Projectors are not focused on groups as a whole. In groups, especially large ones, they most often may feel lost and even disconnected. But even those Projectors who are fine with groups do not interact with the group as a whole, like Generator types can with their enveloping "whirlpool" auras - a Projector's aura focuses on one individual at a time.

I heard some Human Design experts say that a Projector's aura focuses on the G-centre of the other, allowing one to intuitively ask specific questions that may help align the direction of the other. It works even better when the other is a Generator/Manifesting Generator. With their porous open auras, they can really allow the Projector to see within, and the Projector taps into some of their energy in return. Or a lot of energy, which can result in becoming what some call "sacral drunk". You can often observe me getting hyper when I interview Generator guests on my Visibility by Design podcast!

The energy of a Projector's aura is very, very focused. It is laser sharp and quite heavy when locked onto another person that they want to guide. And here is why following the strategy to wait for invitations is so vital!

It is similar to having a personal trainer. Imagine that you are working out, minding your own business and enjoying yourself when suddenly someone comes up to you and starts directing what you should or should not be doing. The first reaction is definitely not a positive one. It is more like, "*Excuse me, WHO are you again?*"

In contrast, if you ask or hire a personal trainer to guide you, then you will trust their vision and expertise. You might actually start pushing and trying harder, breaking through what you thought were your limits.

I often see on social media how Projectors come across as "too heavy" when they offer guidance without an invitation, especially in Human Design groups where people state their energy type. If the recipient does not actually see and recognise this beautiful energy in a specific Projector, it can create all sorts of friction, from resistance to accept advice to completely not acknowledging Projector's gifts and contribution.

Therefore, the strategy for Projector is only to give direct guidance when invited. You need to wait for the invitation from those who see and recognise you as their guide.

That does not affect our visibility activities. We do not need an invitation to create content (more on that later in this chapter). This strategy only affects one on one communication, major life events (relationships, moving houses/countries/environments), and big opportunities.

## Efficiency: Less is More

This is my favourite part. I love doing less and getting as much out of my energy levels as possible. I am a Lifehacker with a capital L. I have no other choice- I am a Projector, after all.

Projectors are superbly gifted with a great sense of systematising and organising things and people to achieve better efficiency. Projectors do not have their Sacral centre defined, which means that even when they are lit up and inspired, they will not have consistent access to the lifeforce energy to take action on it like Generator types do.

This is why Projectors are so good at coming up with efficient ways of doing something. They know that extra effort comes at a price and naturally will find shortcuts and better ways to achieve better results with less effort involved.

As a Projector, I have developed so many efficient shortcuts that save me hours of work. Something that would take me 2 hours before, I can now create in 15 minutes using a system I developed. I have always been like this, but understanding my Human Design explained it so well, so now I am always consciously thinking about how any process can be simplified in a way that is super-efficient with less effort involved. It often comes to a stage where I almost feel guilty for how little I actually 'do" to achieve the results that are traditionally viewed as requiring hard work.

In my business, discovering how to lean into my energetic magnetism unlocked a couple of very consistent client attraction channels that require a minimum amount of effort (mostly one-off focused sessions to create) with a smart optimisation strategy plus automation magic to make them work over and over again.

In fact, it was only when I started focusing on working less in my business in a very effective way that my coaching business started consistently generating reliable and sustainable income levels, even when I had to step back entirely for three months as my husband was terminally ill. Those months ended up being really financially successful, with systems I had created previously that delivered clients and results pretty much on "autopilot."

I do not think I would count on this for the rest of my life because we live in a world that mutates and evolves faster than ever before, so what is working now may not work as well next year. This is why it is important to understand that showing up in your business is not something that can be completely automated.

Plus, energetically speaking, showing up is what is good and healthy for a Projector. For me, the need to show up in my business after my husband passed away was also what helped me heal faster and empowered me to focus on living my life even fuller. The visibility started opening so many more doors, and even this book is a result of me showing up actively and not "hiding" behind the automated part of my marketing. Projectors thrive on live interaction with others. It is what we are here for.

## Self-Recognition

Let's try and understand what activates the abundance flow within a Projector. The signature feeling for a Projector is a feeling of success. And when we feel successful, we create more success in everyone we are here to guide.

But it is a very different feeling to what some Generators may consider success is. I personally do not relate to those stock images with a person on top of the mountain with hands in the air. I mean, come on. As a Classic Projector without any motor centres in my design, I would just be happy the climb is over with - it is exhausting just to write about it! To me, success has nothing to do with doing or achieving anything.

The success feeling is that sweet, sweet sense of being appreciated for that one thing that makes you feel so on purpose, so fulfilled in your role. It only takes someone to truly see us for who we are and acknowledge the breakthroughs we facilitate, often by just being who we are or the guidance we offer. The sweetness is beyond any other reward - one person's recognition at a time.

It is very healthy for a Projector to focus full-heartedly on building their own status and positioning as an authority in their niche - it has much more personally empowering implications. The stronger the status, the more effortless it is to self-recognise and self-appreciate, and the more natural it is to value and love yourself as a Projector.

It's easy to fall into patterns of seeking external validation or recognition from others. Too many Projectors seek that recognition on the outside without focusing on building their own "castle": an environment/opportunity where others can discover, see and recognise them. One of the crucial elements that separate a castle from "any old hut" is the STATUS. The status positions them in a light favourable for recognition and making them available for invitations.

My Projector marketing advice is to always focus on attraction marketing principles: building a strong reputation as a personal brand and focusing on mastering your expertise and showing up and sharing it with the world (focusing within), rather than trying desperately to grab attention (focusing outwards) and proving your worth by doing more for others.

There are days when I feel bored with marketing, or Human Design does not light me up in any way. It is so normal. After all, we are not machines to be on all the time about everything, and we do need to rest and recharge, even from things we love. On those days, I fully allow myself to master other areas I love in my life, like discovering new makeup techniques and lifehacks.

Or I might research the easiest/best/most effective way to [insert anything] - as a Projector, I love finding new ways that make things easier and faster. Or get busy creating something - just for me. Nothing related to business.

I noticed that on those days when I lose myself in irrelevant to my business ventures, I often get new clients reaching out to find out how to work together. When I get into mastering my systems, my internal light is fully on in every area of my life.

In marketing terms, your "castle" could be your website- specifically, the section people can really binge on your content- or your blog. It is also the place where a Projector can create their positioning through all available elements: the content, the visuals, and the credibility markers. And let the status do the "heavy lifting" for you while you focus on creating content around the systems that you master and use in working with clients. Talk about what you feel drawn to, and do not be afraid of repetition.

It is important that we do not create content when we do not feel the need to share something of value with the world. Leaning into what calls you, you can easily draw inspiration for so many interesting points and topics that can be used in your marketing. This is what we should focus on in our content - sharing the topics that mean something poignant to us (perhaps something we see in others) versus trying to say what "they need/want to hear"!

Only by sharing what is burning from within do you give anyone a chance to discover that light, to be drawn to it, to see and recognise your gifts. This is why building your visibility is exactly what you should do as a Projector - it is what your "waiting" looks like. Creating or studying something of true interest to YOU, especially if it is about what you see in the other, produces fabulous strong energy. It is that "losing yourself in the zone as time slows down" kind of magic.

**<u>You are not for everyone, and not everyone is for you!</u>**

When you show up and create this powerful visibility, you will attract people who see you and recognise you, but that is not the end of the process for a Projector. The secret is in practising discernment and learning never to compromise when saying YES to incoming invitations. This means following your Authority, which we will cover later in this book.

Not everyone sees in you what you want them to see. Often people get very excited about something you are good at, but it is not giving you that feeling of deep fulfilment. For example, I have so many really well-sharpened skills in digital marketing, but they do not excite me. Let's assume I am working with a client who raves about one of those "peripheral" talents and whatever the output they produce but completely misses the point of why they work with me as their visibility strategist.

This is not only incorrect, but it is also dangerous for my well-being. As it can make me feel so bitter to realise that they do not "see" me in the same way I desire to be seen, it devalues not just the time and effort I spend with them. It can be detrimental to my self-esteem and self-recognition.

As a Projector, I see myself through the eyes of others. So having people who do not "see" me correctly directly affects how I see myself. Does this make sense?

It is the most insulting and hurtful thing for a Projector not to be recognised for what they want to be recognised for. It feels so unfair, and with that feeling comes resentment and bitterness. The longer or more a Projector "cooks" in that bitter soup, the harder it is to get back to the place where you can shine.

And this means we have to be so careful about accepting invitations, sometimes backtracking, cancelling, and saying NO. It may be a scary thing to do- to fire a client that does not bring you that feeling of success I described earlier but think about the implications.

One client feeding into your bitterness depletes you from the creative sparkle you need to start "getting into the zone." You haven't got the energy to create content for your marketing, as you just don't feel inspired or often confident enough or just feel hurt too much to "shine" your light. You start hiding, hoping to rest and recharge, but that bitterness is not going anywhere. It is physically exhausting, and it bothers you to think about the person who is causing all that. You can even get seriously ill. It is like a very dangerous loop to be stuck in.

So, **thank you, but no, thank you!**

I have been so careful in who I allow into my world these days, and it takes guts. I had to learn to say no without giving an explanation and to set very strong boundaries (even when it feels scary to let others know about them). My world has to be rid of those who I feel are draining my energy, as I know the implications too well.

The last incorrect client in my business was the cause of so much lost revenue, simply by impacting me in a way where I was reluctant and almost afraid to attract any more people like that... As a result, I simply did not launch. I couldn't make myself promote my one-on-one coaching offers, and I stopped making myself available for private clients.

Do not get me wrong, there is nothing "wrong" with that client at the heart of this story, for they are a wonderful person in their own expression, but it was a very incorrect relationship for me.

I believe that it is by learning to only accept correct invitations and adjust your current relationships in the way that feels correct that a Projector feel creative, successful, and fulfilled. Correctness is the secret! Which means inner strength and valuing yourself and your gifts above "people pleasing."

**You are not for everyone, and not everyone is for you!**

I think this has become a mantra for me in the last couple of years. A mantra that continues ridding my life of those who have no place in it and making me aware of when somehow the incorrectness crept in again, so I can re-align, transforming my life.

## Projector's Energy Levels

One of the common traits when we talk about Projectors is to say that Projectors have no energy to consistently "do" or create, but it is only partially true. Projectors are the most diverse type (except for Reflectors- each one is literally unique from the rest), and this means that some Projectors have very different experiences with their energy levels than others.

Based on the definition in their design, Projectors can be divided into three groups: Mental Projectors (nothing below their Throat Centre is defined), Energy Projectors (one or more of their motor centres - Will, Emotional, Root- are defined, but not connected to their Throat centre which would make them Manifestors), and Classic Projectors (Spleen and/or G-centre defined). The lives of these three groups are very different from each other, and so are their energy levels. Their physical and creative energy levels are very different.

Looking at an Energy Projector, for example, there is that force trying to get to the throat from one of the motor centres, and often they would be acting almost like Manifestors, initiating themselves and others into action. (Just remember that you are still NOT Manifestors, and follow your strategy to wait for invitations!) This energy will come in waves or pulses depending on the motors in their chart, and they can learn to anticipate and manage these patterns.

While some Mental Projectors, like my daughter, Chantelle, might eagerly identify with a "permanently exhausted pigeon" on their best days. Their whole lifestyle, as well as how they approach running their business and showing up in their marketing will be drastically different from Energy Projectors. This makes the statement that Projectors have no energy somewhat out of touch with reality. Some do, some don't.

The real questions for any Projector are:

• Do you follow your strategy to wait for invitations before you enter relationships and opportunities?

• What do you need to do while you are waiting?

• How discerning are you with the invitations that come in?

To answer these questions, we need to understand the mechanics behind how Projectors' auras interact with others, the concept of correctness, and how to set the stage for correct invitations to come into their lives without pushing, grabbing, kicking, and screaming bitterly into the abyss. I hope this section has given you some answers.

## Visibility For Projectors (And all other types, in fact!)

Now you know that as a Projector, a strategy to "wait for invitations" is all about setting up the stage for those invitations to come in and then being very discerning about accepting the correct ones.

I already mentioned that you do not need to wait to be invited to create content. As long as you are creating when you are "in the zone" and not to "be visible," - your content in any form you choose will be energetically backed up.

What happens when you create content for the sake of being visible is that you are just creating more noise to put out there. It may be written well, explain your point well, and have a perfect CTA, but it is energetically empty. It is what people scroll by on social media. Why? Because you are not doing it to shine your light. You are just trying to "fill the gap" in your content strategy. Talking for the sake of talking.

Only create content when you are really feeling the desire to talk about a specific point that you are so passionate about at the time.

Since Projectors do not have the energy to be endlessly "in the zone," my advice is to allow yourself to NOT be producing content consistently. Forget blocking off time to create your posts. Jot down ideas and insights that come to you on your client calls or walks in the park. As long as you do have the discipline to actually record that video or write that post when you are feeling the creative juice flowing - you will be able to re-energise yourself and let your light shine through your words like a lighthouse.

There are numerous ways to create a very consistent visibility that serves you perfectly without hustling all the time. It is about the bigger picture, about understanding how your business operates.

Start with getting clear on how the stranger who finds a piece of your content can become a client (provided they are the correct person or an ideal client, as they like to call it in traditional marketing). What steps do they need to take after reading your post, your blog, or listening to a podcast episode you spoke at? Is it easy for them to take these steps? Are these steps making it faster and easier for YOU to be available for an invitation to guide them or into any other exciting opportunities they may bring? How can you make an aligned decision if the invitations are correct? All of this is part of the consideration when deciding on your marketing funnels and business models in general.

Talking about consistent content, there are so many things we could be adding into the mix that we often overlook. For example, posting client testimonials, promoting our lead magnets, posting direct invitations to our offers, or reusing content created "in the zone" in the past to serve you again and again - with automation.

I love using automation to promote podcast episodes I was featured on, the articles on my blog, and some nurturing posts about my insights around visibility and how understanding even the basic level of your Human Design can empower you to show up. Each one of these categories has a specific "bucket" in my automation tool. In fact, part of my content strategy process is to add a piece of content I just created (or was featured on) to the bottom of my automated content category, so it can be reposted on all my social media channels in a few weeks and then again in a few weeks.

Driving traffic back to my website, where people can binge on more of my goodness, is the main focus. In a world of noise, one way to get noticed is by repeating what you already said before. Once is never enough, but for a Projector's marketing, this principle is very, very handy. Create, then automate.

As long as you are creating when energetically lit up ("in the zone"), this piece of content will attract the correct people to you again and again - and again. That is exactly how I was able to let my marketing bring clients into the business on autopilot in the last three months of my husband's life journey - without me creating a single new post. I simply couldn't. But my previous work, the "castle" I have been building, became a fort that could protect me from failing to show up in my business when I needed to step back.

Projectors' marketing requires a longer-term vision. While being grateful for wins along the way, it is always about building a stronger foundation through sharing that light powerfully when you can - so it can continue shining when you need time off. The one thing to remember, and I cannot repeat it often enough: **YOU DO NOT NEED TO BE INVITED INTO BEING VISIBLE.** It is being visible that brings correct invitations to you. Focus on being visible - and work with your energy patterns and natural rhythms. **For more insights, invite me to guide you at marketingbyhumandesign.com**

# Chapter Nine

# Reflectors: Here To Be Different

## Sample, Digest & Reflect.

When it comes to the Reflector type, we are entering a very different "domain." You see, no Reflector is like the other Reflector. It is the most diverse energy type as each one of those Reflectors is a unique being. What makes Reflector a separate type is the complete absence of defined centres in their chart. There are some gates here and there, but no channels connecting and defining centres on each side. This makes each individual Reflector very different in the way they experience life. And if you are a Reflector, understanding how to approach and embrace this uniqueness is key to self-empowerment and alignment for you. You will never feel like there is something wrong with you again, and learn how to take advantage of this life experience and your role through your business.

The question you are here to ask is simple: WHO IS DIFFERENT? You are designed the way you are, as unique as you are, for a reason. You are blessed with a gift to see what is different in the other. You are here to observe, sample, digest, and then share what you see. But it is not about who YOU are. When you try to figure yourself out, trying to find out who you are, or worse, trying to be like everyone else - you get lost and often will think something is wrong with you.

So, don't waste time in this beautiful life - focus on what you are experiencing and who is in your aura - who is different from the world around them? You can spot those who are different and can so clearly see their potential. You can see who "exited the Matrix" - and for you, it is about allowing yourself to be different, too, your unique self.

## Identity & Authenticity

Reflectors make up about 1% of the population and are said to have a heightened sensitivity to their environment and the people around them. They are highly intuitive and adaptable, as well as capable of having a deep understanding of others. Without defined centres, there is not that much-fixed energy to rely on (although it is important to note that the theme of their Incarnation Cross and their Profile lines will definitely add a certain flavour to life's journey).

I also think it is very important that when we use the word energy, we really distinguish between the physical energy and the energies in terms of themes and traits. Although Reflectors would be referred to as a non-energy type, this does not necessarily say they cannot have a lot of physical energy. In fact, a Reflector would become a different type most days of the lunar cycle.

So, let's talk about this cycle a little to understand what happens to a Reflector. While all other types (99% of the population) are affected more by the Solar activity in their chart, the Reflector is much more affected by the Lunar activity. As the moon in their chart travels along the astrological wheel, spending every 8-12 hours in different gates, this directly affects a Reflector's real-life experiences. It is very beneficial if you are a Reflector to gain a little more knowledge and awareness of the lunar transits through these gates to observe and make notes of your experience and themes throughout the lunar cycle.

Every day, a transit activates something in Reflector's design, often making them live as a different energy type for the day. It is so interesting because. When it comes to making decisions, a Reflector can only be sure after they experience a full cycle of activations in their body. I will cover this in the section on Decision Making. Reflectors' brand identity and voice may and will change over time, and embracing this fluidity is perfect for them.

I am personally very fond of looking at daily transits, maybe because, as a Projector, I am, just like Reflectors, a non-energy type. Some days, I act as a Manifesting Generator - I notice that this shows in me switching from one task to another a lot and yet completing everything perfectly by the end of the day. On the other day, I could be a Manifestor or a Generator. Every flavour adds its nuances.

This is ninja-level stuff, of course, and I would not have the expertise to educate you about this, but the bottom line is that it can explain your natural life patterns. When you have some awareness of these patterns, you can also work around and take advantage of the themes for your benefit.

For you, every day of the lunar cycle sees you changing as the planets are moving through the sky, activating themes and energy in your design. You can be living 10000 lifetimes in 24 hours. It is a very special experience; I am in awe of it even as I write this now... And this creates that specific unique experience for you. You are not here to find out who you are- you are everything, and everything is you. So magical and yet, so real.

Another important aspect is other people's auras. As a Reflector, you literally sample, digest, and reflect the energies of others - without identifying with these energies as your own. Often a Reflector can jump from one thing they get obsessed with to another, from one belief to another. It can feel like they are inconsistent or perhaps lack the ability to stick to something, questioning their authenticity throughout this process. This is a common theme for a Reflector, yet one thing to surrender to is that this IS your authentic self.

As an empath, who experiences the energy of others on such a deep level, this exploration process is what makes you authentic. **You do not need to become attached to a belief or a set identity as you sample them.**

When we look at the role of a Reflector to sample and reflect its environment, it makes so much sense that after sampling an idea, an activity, or an interest, a Reflector develops an insight they need to know what it is about, but they are free not to take everything they come across as their identity. A Reflector exists beyond set identity, so to speak.

In marketing, I think this is quite cool if you, as a Reflector, give yourself permission to go into anything that draws you to sample it and then let go of it and move to whatever draws you next without self-shame, or trying to stick to something out of fear of being judged.

Through this process, you are building up so many insights into what we are as humanity. Your insights and wisdom deliver so much essence that others may miss. You are a kind of "oracle" that people come to for advice, and you can naturally see what is good for them or where they do not live out their full potential. This is your role, and to gain that wisdom, you need to move through concepts and experiences without being stuck in them.

## Community

Due to having no fixed energies in their design, Reflectors are here to be the product of their environment. Often a Reflector will be a great indicator of the "health" of the environment and people around them. This means that as a Reflector, you need to be very careful who you allow in your world because you will always be affected by the definition and conditioning of those around you.

Again, this all makes sense since you are sampling the environment and reflecting whatever you pick up back at it. Sometimes it may be difficult for people to deal with you, reflecting their lower frequencies on them. This is why you need to be mindful of who you are hanging around with.

With your marketing and business, this is especially vital. The quality of the communities you are part of is paramount, for you will pick up and reflect back all the good as well as all the bad and ugly that is around you. Try stepping back from the drama and curating who is allowed in your world. The challenge for you is that sometimes you are not sensing that toxicity in the environment as it consumes you. My personal advice? Step back and try reflecting upon what NOT being part of the community feels like to you. You may have some surprising insights. And SURPRISE is your signature feeling of alignment. Your journey in life is to be surprised by all that the world has to offer (and not disappointed by it).

It will be beneficial for you to set boundaries and define who you welcome into your inner circle, and curate your own communities in a way that does not allow negativity. Whilst promoting flexibility and open-mindedness.

## Reflectors in Business & Marketing

Reflectors make amazing coaches simply because, due to their unique design, they can allow some of the conditioning from other people in as a "sample," and then they can communicate what they see back. This really helps with the deconditioning process, breaking through limiting beliefs, and decluttering the path to fulfilling the potential within. Reflectors can emphasise and hold space for the others they are face to face with. They can really see deep into the other person and see their potential.

Where the hiccups can happen is with the implementation of business strategies and the consistency with that implementation. The key point to understand here is that the uniqueness of each Reflector's design creates a sort of pressure to figure out things. It happens mostly by trying, testing, and discovering what feels right over a Lunar cycle - and, most importantly, not trying to run their business the way everyone else does.

With such a unique design, how can we expect something generic to work? My advice, give yourself permission to "do it your way" and focus on sampling, trying, and testing various things for at least a month (even better over three months), as it will bring a better understanding of what is working and what is not; especially how it feels through a few lunar cycles.

And, of course, with online visibility, my advice to a Reflector would also be to focus on attraction marketing and create evergreen content (video, long-form written) when lit up/in the zone. Express what you see in the world around you and then perhaps tap into some tools that will help to automate the rotating repurposing of this content. This will give you some breathing space and remove the need to hustle on social media all the time, which can lead to a go/stop type of energy. Create consistent visibility with possibly automated quality content, which keeps nurturing and converting readers into followers. If they are the correct people for you, eventually, they will turn into clients.

Success is not about posting on Instagram every day - even if everyone in the world says this is how you do it. Success for everyone looks very different, even when it seems the same at a glance. Online marketing is a noisy space, and the louder someone is, the more convincing they often come across... but it is not THE TRUTH for you. You are here to figure out YOUR WAY and find YOUR TRUTH in marketing, in business, and in life. **For more guidance, do not hesitate to visit marketingbyhumandesign.com**

# Part Three

## What is Correct For You

# Chapter Ten

# The Magic Of Aligned Decisions

## Your Authentic Choices

The next area where Human Design is invaluable is making decisions. It is generally life-changing, and smart business decisions help create a solid foundation for growth. What strategy to use, who to listen to, to launch or not to launch, what email sequence would convert more readers- all those questions and more require deciding on. Yet, with Human Design Authority, you can ensure that your decisions are correct for you. They are not made out of lack, FOMO (the fear of missing out), or simply because you think you should do something because that is "the way" they do it.

I love the comparison of Human Design Authority to your inner judgment to do as you see right for you, following your true desires and motives, and not allowing your Mind, Ego, or other people in your life to influence or derail you from your True Path. Yet not everyone has the same way their Authority shows. It is fascinating actually to explore and experience yours.

This is one area that will allow you the most alignment: not just in your business but in life in general. The correct decisions are never made from the Mind. Your Mind is there to get inspired, ask questions, rationalise, research, and evaluate. Yet, it is too hooked up (and often believes) in the conditioning you receive. Your Mind has no access to your innate wisdom, the mechanism that your unique Design offers for making decisions about what is correct and what is incorrect for YOU. It is your energetics, your Authority, that is truly in control. Unless you allow your Authority to guide you, you will always face making misaligned decisions out of your Mind and regretting them later.

Discovering, practising, and then knowing how your body responds when you make a decision will give you freedom and security. It will guide you on what content to create, who to engage with, whose programs to invest in, and whom you allow into your own business, and all of that is very empowering.

An important marketing note: your Authority does not dictate creating content and expressing yourself through it to attract clients. But it absolutely will influence who you follow, engage with, hire, or take on as a client in your business. Just as much as any opportunities presented to you in your business - always follow your Strategy and Authority to enter the correct ones for you without overthinking.

In this section, as a reference point, I am using the work of Richard Rudd, who is a great teacher most known for developing the Gene Keys system. I, however, absolutely adore the work he did with Ra Uru Hu on Human Design. In my research so far, he has given the most comprehensive definitions and easy-to-follow advice, especially when it comes to Human Design authorities. Therefore, I will follow his breakdown of the Inner Authorities into groups and follow his direction for describing various authorities expressed through different energy Types.

Chapter Eleven

# Emotional Authority

## No Truth in Spontaneity

This is the most common Authority. Around half of the population falls into this group - which makes every second in the world an Emotional Authority person. If you have the Solar Plexus Centre coloured in your chart - you fall into this group. Emotional power is very dominant, so it doesn't even matter what other centres you have defined. These emotional waves will always take over the "voices" of other centres. You need to get clear in your emotions when making a decision. Not too elated and not too "angry with the world" (my Emotional Generator sister came up with this wonderful expression to describe her emotional lows).

Emotional Authority comes from the defined Emotional (Solar Plexus) Centre and operates in waves. Some waves build up slowly and go down slowly. Some waves build up powerfully and then crash suddenly. Some resemble a pulse in its manifestation. It all depends on your Design specifics. Even though this is a bit of a "ninja-level," - I think you will appreciate taking a few minutes to look into what emotional waves are more familiar to you. But frankly, you do not need to know the gate number or what it represents to tune within over time and see what kind of waves you tend to experience. The most important takeaway here is to become aware of them.

Since you are dealing with constant ups and downs, highs and lows, it is very unreliable to make a decision in a moment. Waiting to get through the emotional wave to the point of emotional clarity can be quite challenging. It is a great example of how conditioning works- when we tend to be always pulled towards the opposite of what is good for us, believing that it is the "right" way.

The Solar Plexus Centre is also a motor centre. It gives the owner energy to take action, and this is why it is very tricky to resist for people with Emotional Authority. They are constantly pushed into taking action by this motor, and yet the emotions can cloud that inner judgment. The bottom line and the strategy for an Emotional Authority person is to avoid impulsive actions and make informed decisions, especially when it comes to important choices in life. Ironically, most people with Emotional Authority who have not been experimenting with Human Design actually love being spontaneous and making decisions in a moment - a great illustration of the influence of a motor centre.

Yet, very often, an Emotional Authority person will later regret a decision made in the moment. Things and circumstances change, their mood changes, and they have to deal with something that they agreed to, but it does not feel right. The key is to watch, recognise, and really master waiting through your emotional waves.

Let these waves work themselves out over time. It is healthy and CORRECT for you to "think about it" or to be indecisive, even when you need to make up your mind there and then. For example, in a restaurant, you can change your mind many times. You should be the last one to order because as you look at the menu, you are feeling through every dish and might need to come back to some of them again and feel differently about them. In fact, Richard Rudd mentions that people with Emotional Authority are likely to have issues with eating too much because they tend to eat when they feel they want to. If only they wait to follow this feeling through, they will discover if it is genuine hunger or if this feeling will just dissipate and disappear.

This could apply to choosing your strategies and your tools in marketing, especially with getting excited about buying a particular software. This is where trials and money-back guarantees are so vital for you. Waiting to see if the desire actually to use it is still there after a day or two, if it is as easy as you thought, or does what you actually need to do. Trust me, indecision is great for you and will save you a lot of money. The same applies to hiring a coach. Never do it on the discovery call, no matter how much they are offering to knock off the price if you sign up there and then. Personally, that approach is a red flag for me as it gives zero control to make a correct decision, no matter what Authority we have. Take a day or so to feel through your feeling and if you are still feeling good about hiring that person or a company - go for it.

The beauty of following your Authority on any decision is that you can be sure that even if things do not work out - if you follow your Authority, you will be learning an invaluable lesson from this experience, something that can give you more clarity in the long run. For an Emotional Authority person, being spontaneous and jumping into things headfirst can only add friction, overwhelm, and the rest of the "funky bunch" of negative experiences that could be easily avoided if only you fell in love with waiting. Waiting is a huge factor in Human Design for everyone, and we will discuss it further in this book.

Another crucial element to understand here is how important TIME is for you. Imagine a wave - either a wave in the sea or a sound wave. A wave is essentially something that changes constantly over time. And this in itself explains why being "in the moment" or spontaneous is not for you. It is not reliable. You need to allow this wave to change, to run its course. There is a build-up, followed by a crash/descent (happy/sad, hope/pain). These waves inspire action. They help you gain awareness of your emotional state at every moment. Emotional clarity usually happens somewhere at the end of the wave as you go through the whole process. Emotional awareness is not just about one moment, it is about the whole process.

How long you should wait depends on how experienced you are with your emotional awareness. I know some people who practice breath-work and other techniques to get to their emotional clarity faster, and some say it should be a 24-hour period. I don't have emotional Authority to report first-hand, but my observation is that it really depends on what your decision is about and also how new it is to you. If there is something you have been thinking about for a bit, chances are you have already gone through your emotional wave around it. If this is something completely new, you need to give yourself a little time before committing. I think this is the wisest approach - and as you practice watching your emotions, you will begin to determine the best waiting period for you.

Remember, there is no right or wrong in Human Design. It is about you experimenting and finding your most natural ways.

By the way, as a side note - your mood will affect those around you, whether they want it or not. So be mindful of your influence, especially of your low wave, as it can condition those in your presence to feel low or even take your mood as a personal insult or accusation.

This was me with my sister for 40 years, and it felt like a personal attack. When I realised, she was an Emotional Authority driven person. It was like a huge weight fell off my shoulders. It gave me permission not to feel bad when she was moody. But this only works because I am aware and consciously working on letting go of her emotional influence - it is still very palpable for me. I wanted to add this side note because it is not all about trying to decondition from external influence but also to see how taking personal responsibility for how we can condition others is crucial, especially with such a powerful energy as that of an Emotional Centre.

## Emotional Authority Summary

**Patience is a virtue!**

**Don't let your decisions be ruled by your passions, no matter how strong, beautiful, or certain you feel. When you don't rush into things, they work out in the most beautiful way, and over time following your Authority can alter the rhythm of life for you as you stop jumping into things and making commitments you later regret.**

# Chapter Twelve

# Sacral (Fluid) Authority

## Your Body Always Knows

This next Authority only applies to Generators and Manifesting Generators that do not have the Emotional Centre defined and therefore do not deal with emotional waves in order to get clear. It is an "in the moment" gut feeling, better described as the feeling flowing up your body from your gut. It is generated in your Sacral Centre, which can be likened to an in-built GPS that tells you where to "turn". It operates through a YES/NO response and very often even shows itself through subconscious mumbling sounds. But we are not taught as children to tune into our bodies, so often, these reactions get completely ignored.

My Mom is a Sacral Authority Generator, and when I ask her something, and she says YES, often I see in the subtle way she sighs or quivers her mouth that her body is saying NO. Mom is in her 80s now. She is not someone who has any awareness of her Strategy or Authority by Human Design, so she is a great example for me of someone who is super conditioned (Generators tend to be very conditioned), people-pleasing and not following her Sacral responses, often ending up in disappointment and failed expectations. If only she had discovered the power to trust that her body always knows what is good for her - so many things, including the satisfaction she could get out of life, her marriage, and her social life, could have been so much more satisfying.

Remember what I wrote about checking in with your Sacral if you have the available energy for this or that? This awareness is crucial for you and will make following your Sacral Responded in a very easy, almost laid-back way. No frustration or guilting yourself for being "selfish" -you simply have no energy available for what you are asked or need to doc at that moment, and that is the end of that!

The Sacral responds to the life on the outside of you. It is the only Authority that does not come from the place of awareness - which means it is an automatic mechanism, and it is working for you, constantly responding to the outside world ALL THE TIME. You do not have to "think" about your decisions. You may find you say YES easily to so many things when you feel it. (Because your Sacral's job is to say YES to things that are correct for it). You may find that when presented with a Yes or No question, it is much easier for you to know what to choose rather than having a multiple choice. Again, this is the nature of Sacral Response.

Try practising listening to your gut and watching it light up with a juicy "*Oh yes!*" or withdrawing with an "*ugh*" when something feels wrong. Sometimes it might even grunt or moan, even though it is not a "Vocal" Authority. You might be leaning forward when it is a Yes and backward when you do not like something. Try observing yourself over a period of time, and you will find out how your body likes to respond, and then you can become more and more familiar with these response sensations.

Follow those reactions and do not try to explain them or override them with what "should" be done. Sometimes these reactions are very subtle, and you need to practice listening, but over time, you will get more and more in tune with your body. Only through the Sacral

Response can you make a reliable decision.

Another note: as opposed to the Splenic Authority that I will talk about next, which also has some body sensations (if you have your Splenic Centre defined, you will often be feeling them too), a Sacral authority overrides any other sensations for your decision making, so try to focus on identifying the feeling of your Response.

Rudd explains, "*Your inner response can be felt or heard as an inner voice or an impulse that almost seems to move through you, rather than coming from you. This is known as 'living in the response field.' The more you can wait in life, and the less you worry, the more you can relax and attune to these internal impulses that will always tell you exactly what is right for you.*"

Your Master Key with the Sacral Authority is to "Follow your Flow." Richard Rudd calls the Sacral Authority group "The Fluid" Authority group, and I absolutely love the choice of the word here.

There are a couple of things you need to be aware of with this Authority. One is being too emotional, stressed, or too excited by anything that can "cloud" the sound of your responses. The other is all about other people. When another person is in your aura, they can condition you - through chemistry and general presence- and then you can mistake feeling good in this person's presence for your Sacral response. Be aware of spontaneous decisions in other people's presence. Ideally, you need to be out of their aura to hear your Sacral response.

The feeling of flow is something that indicates that you are making correct decisions and choices. Often something major can feel so natural. This is what we call "the Flow of Life." Things just fall into place, as if by magic, with a feeling of certainty deep inside. On the other hand, incorrect decisions will cause resistance and more stress and frustration.

Being in the rhythm with the flow of life is crucial for you. When you are pressured by someone, it can disturb your rhythm and even derail you, so make your rhythm a priority. As we learned, the pace and the rhythm will be different for a Generator and a Manifesting Generator, so determining your "lane" and being empowered and "ok" with sticking to your specific pace of living is crucial for you.

With Manifesting Generators, there is one difference that Rudd spotted and that I did not see mentioned anywhere else (or perhaps, I simply missed it, as we are all human, after all).

While a Sacral (Pure) Generator can feel the response and know immediately if it is a Yes or a No, a Sacral Manifesting Generator has a secret second response that is even more crucial to gain awareness about.

That second response will only happen when a Manifesting Generator starts doing what they responded positively to at first. For example, you see a comment in a Facebook group asking about something you are an expert at. You feel an internal flow - a YES to the topic and decide to write an article about it.

If you are a Manifesting Generator, what can happen is when you open a new Google doc (or whatever you use) to start writing, suddenly you get the "*ugh*" response in your body. This means that it is perhaps not the time to focus on writing OR even the topic you actually want to create an article about.

Follow that second response, as you are designed to follow your internal urges and shift direction much more swiftly than a Generator, so do not shame yourself for not being able to "stick to it." Do it when and only AS you are lit up about whatever you are doing. If not, get back to it later.

## Sacral Authority Summary

**Find your natural flow!**

**Resistance is a good indication that you went off your path and need to get back in touch with your flow. Generally, making decisions is easy and natural for you - almost automatic - but emotions or other people can affect you in a way that is confusing and stops you from being clear and at ease with your decisions.**

# Chapter Thirteen

# Splenic (Instinctive) Authority

## The Whispers of Truth

We arrive at my Authority ruled by the Spleen Centre - the centre of physical awareness underpinned by our immune system. It is about feeling safe or unsafe, and this Authority is, just like the Sacral, the opposite of the Emotional one. It is all about what we feel in the moment.

This is not a loud overpowering Authority, and it takes time to learn how it shows in your body, as different people report different body sensations. Another caveat is that the voice of the Spleen is very quiet. Most of the time, it communicates through sensations, although when it wants to warn you against great danger, it can show itself in visions and even a voice - but only in extremely dangerous situations.

A quick story of a warning was when I decided to borrow a bit of caustic soda from the place where I worked to unblock a pipe at home. I don't think I even realised that caustic soda is a type of acid. So, I poured some into a plastic Coke bottle. As I was pouring it, I had a vision of looking down at my long black coat and seeing it covered in purple chemical streaks... On my way home, I popped into a few shops. As I was walking around, I had a feeling people were staring at me. A few minutes later, outside, I spotted another weird look on a by-passers face. He was looking at my bottom half. I glanced down and saw the purple streaks from the vision earlier. The acid had eaten through the bottle, through my bag, through my coat and my trousers!!!

I really do not know how I did not end up with a chemical burn on my leg. A miracle I will forever be grateful for, as I also will be for the porter in a guest house around the corner where I was, who didn't kick me out when I ran in and demanded to take a shower. Instead, he helped me dispose of all the acid and everything that it damaged, let me shower, gave me a pair of pants, and called me a taxi. God bless him and his kindness. I literally had to peel my trousers from my skin in that shower.

Splenic Authority can also warn you about a life-changing "dreams come true" moment. I experience it as a flutter between my collarbones. In 2019, just before my daughter's name was called out as a winner of the Trinity College Dublin Scholar Nomination, I felt that tremble in my chest, like I had an enormous butterfly trapped in there, and then the announcer said, "*Chantelle Esper for Theoretical Physics.*" That award was nothing short of winning a 100K lottery - it gave her an amazing start to her academic career with a 5-year scholarship, accommodation right in the heart of Trinity College campus, and Harry Potter-style meals at the Commons every day. Wow, what a day, what an achievement! And my body knew she got it before anyone else did.

Exactly the same thing happened when my husband's music production project called Amasis was nominated for a New Act 2010 on Meteor Ireland Music awards (it is sort of an Irish Grammy's event). This was a brand-new band with no fans or following, and the winners were chosen by public votes - so we had little chance of winning. Just before the winner was announced, I KNEW with my whole body it was Amasis, against all odds. And I was, of course, correct!

It also works for me in marketing and business. The first reactions, first impressions, and following what I feel in the moment have changed the way I do everything. And here is why: THERE IS NO LOGIC TO SPLENIC RESPONSES, but they are always correct!

However, this creates a huge mental issue because the Mind cannot explain your inner knowing, and it creates so much confusion. There is a great danger of "talking yourself into it" and going against your intuitive guidance. And since the Splenic voice is quiet - the Mind wins quite often, thus leading you towards something completely incorrect for you. It may be a good idea to prioritise first impressions and instincts, and if you are feeling "off" about something, follow that feeling without trying to explain it logically.

How to deal with that? Remember that Splenic is a very primal Authority. Animals often make decisions based on their gut feeling and definitely not after considering pros and cons. Following their instinct means more chances of survival. Splenic Authority is in charge of your survival, and it does not need the interference of the Mind to try and find an explanation. It literally just KNOWS. That feeling of knowing is how I would describe it. It is slightly different from the Sacral Authority, which also manifests physically, but in the form of flowing through the body.

The Spleen can also communicate through specific physical sensations. On my podcast interviews and client calls, when I say or hear something that is aligned with my clients or me, I get very distinct tingles - often even goosebumps on my upper arms. When I get that feeling - I know it is right for me to follow the direction or idea we discussed. When something is incorrect for me, I get a tightening in the base of my throat, and often hairs stand up on the back of my neck.

Another way the Spleen shows up is with the specific taste in my mouth- a sweetness when it is a positive and metallic for a negative reaction. These taste changes seem to be common amongst Splenic people. Try watching your own sensations and tastes to figure out your own Splenic cues.

Splenic Authority is highly unpredictable, but what it wants is what your body wants and needs. Even in business, it is about following your instincts when consuming "information" or taking action, which looks completely different from the conditioned traditional way of "how to run your business." For example, you can never have a schedule or plan your activities too far ahead. When the moment comes to follow the next stage of the plan, you might feel very differently about it. So, in a way committing to some sort of pre-planned schedule could be an issue.

In my personal Design, I also have a completely open Will centre, which means I should not make any promises or commitments. There could be some factors in your Design that will allow you to have a more structured approach to your work.

Lastly, it's important to know that Splenic Authority doesn't talk all the time (like a Sacral Authority, which responds to everything in each moment). It does not repeat itself, either, so you have to act in the moment or not at all. Hesitation can only allow the Mind to interfere - but the Spleen is not interested in arguing. It will just go quiet again. It speaks once, and it is final.

When you feel a sense of danger about something - for example, you were invited to feature your online course in a product bundle, but you feel that "off" feeling - decline and do not look back. Who knows, maybe it is warning you off getting exposed to the incorrect audience or risking undermining your brand reputation as you may not realise that you are entering a misaligned promotion style. Or someone you do not want to be associated with could also be part of that bundle.

The main thing is not to second guess your instinct. You will not know WHY most of the time. And since you followed your intuition and declined the offer, you will never find out. BE OK WITH THAT!

Watch your body's responses. If your intuition tells you to leave a group of people, leave it (make up an excuse if you need to). If your intuition tells you something is off about the person on the discovery call - do not offer them to work with you, no matter how much money they are prepared to throw at you. You will pay a higher price if you enter a relationship with an incorrect person, and your Authority will always warn you against what is unhealthy for you. But you must quieten your Mind and listen.

By the way, Splenic people are often considered somewhat cool and even cold at times, but this, again, in my opinion, has to do with that animal nature; awareness is always over emotions. In fact, I call myself a "flat liner," emotionally speaking, and I am OK with it. At the end of the day, how can one make any correct decisions when they are emotional anyway?

## Splenic Authority Summary

**Trust your spontaneous instincts!**

**There is no logic, and you will need to have full faith in yourself and your inner guidance through first impressions in any decision. Hesitation is your worst enemy. As you lean into your primal gut feeling, you will start seeing the correctness and how strong and sharp your instincts are.**

# Chapter Fourteen

# Volitional Authority Group

## Follow Your Heart

Rudd divided this group into Self-Manifested (something I haven't come across before), Ego-Projected and Ego-Manifested Authorities. Statistically speaking, these are very rare. The decision-making in this group is focused on the Will Centre (also called the Ego or the Heart centre), and it is all about having the willpower to make the commitment and follow through. Watch for the commitments that come out of your mouth without the need for any forethought - what you say you will or have to do. Remember, it's healthy for you to make promises that you keep. Follow what you SAY you will do (and not what you think you should do).

As the name suggests, this is the Authority group where what you want and desire determines your truth. It is all about having the willpower to make the commitment and follow through, and each authority has its own flavour.

The Will centre is also a motor that works in work/rest - work/rest patterns. If you belong to this decision-making group and have the willpower, the desire, and the wanting to do something, you get to activate that "work" mode and tap into its energy to complete the process. If your heart's not in it, you will never be able to follow through. Learn to appreciate the rest periods that allow you to recharge and learn not to push it when the motor is resting.

The Will Centre carries a very powerful charge. It can often be misunderstood as selfishness or self-obsession, but don't let this stop you from being who you are. This is the fuel for making correct decisions for you, and it will charge you with determination and willpower that provokes unease in others, but that is their "business," not yours. People with these Authorities are often much more sensitive than others may assume, so being misunderstood can perhaps make you want to be softer or lenient, but that is not what you are born to be. Lean into your Type's Strategy to ensure you are operating correctly but trust your desires and where they take you.

An important note: it is healthiest and safest for you to make decisions alone and in complete solitude. When others are in your energy field, they can easily condition, disturb or influence you with their emotional state. You should also watch your own emotional state and never make decisions when nervous or excited.

## Ego Manifested Authority

This Authority, defined by the Will centre that is connected directly to your Throat, allows you as a Manifestor to express your desires and needs through your words. For the Ego Manifested Manifestor, your needs often manifest as *"I want...," "I need...," "I don't want,"* or *"I don't need... "* and that's your Truth.

But society has this thing where it encourages us to ask for our needs rather than boldly stating them. It's like they prefer a polite request over a strong declaration. But here's the thing: all this conditioning can really mess with the inner authority of a Manifestor. It's a real challenge that calls for a major mindset shift to reclaim that true power you possess.

You must resist filtering your words when seeking your truth. Your speech is fuelled by an internal non-verbal, creative flow, and it naturally responds to whether you have the resources available to fully commit to what is being asked of you.

When you decline an opportunity, it's because you genuinely lack the resources to commit to the task or project fully. It could also be that you don't find yourself interested in investing your energy into that particular endeavour.

Trust your inner knowing and honour your boundaries when it comes to choosing where to direct your precious energy. Being a non-Sacral being, it's crucial for you to prioritise having sufficient rest and replenishment cycles before taking on new ventures.

You are born to be your own boss; it is just something that is part of you. You have an innate ability to make money in whatever you do, but calling your own shots is going to feel most aligned for you. You will do whatever you need best if you do it on your own. It does not mean that you need to work on completing everything you start, but more about designing what you make money from in a way that gives you flexibility and freedom from dependency on others.

Even if you have a team, make sure you are not the one that manages the projects. You need the space to do your thing the way you desire. Just make sure you inform others on your path by just stating what you are about to do. This will remove unease and resistance and get people on board when you need to.

## Self-Manifested Authority

This is an extremely rare Authority, so much so that it does not get mentioned in any standard Human Design literature. After I came across Rudd's mention of this Authority, I went on an extensive search for more information, as in his source, he did not specify what exactly determines this Authority in one's design. Eventually, I found out that this refers to a design of a Manifestor where the Will centre is connected to the G-centre (known as the Identity centre), which makes this Self Manifested Authority all about SELF-LOVE.

Your correct decisions will be driven by the desire to do something as an act of self-love - just make sure you inform those involved or on your path.

As a Self-Manifested Manifestor, your Authority in Human Design is incredibly rare and unique. With your ego centre connected to your identity centre, you have the power to ask yourself a crucial question whenever you make decisions: *"Am I doing this because I REALLY WANT TO?"*

Self-Manifested Authority is all about having the courage to pursue what brings you joy in life. It's about embracing a sense of self-centredness without any guilt. You are here to carve a path that no one else has ever walked before.

I only found one Self-Manifested Manifestor that knows about her design in the online visibility space - the creator of Femme CEO and business coach Laura Niese. For a while, Laura could not identify with the description of Ego Manifested Authority, but when she discovered Rudd's work and his explanation of Self-Manifested Authority, it made total sense.

Laura shared, *"I was called selfish more than once in my life, but now I know that this authority is, in fact, all about being SELFish. You have to check in with yourself and see if your decision is something you want to do - in a very selfish way. I discovered that it evokes anger when I abandon mySELF to people please, even if I genuinely try to make someone else happy or do something I think I 'should' do but do not want to. Even when I try to hide the anger and try to engage fully, people involved can sense clearly that I just don't want to be there, and it can be so repelling. As a Manifestor, I know anger is a signature feeling of misalignment, and I already have the repelling aura. Making decisions that do not include checking in with what I actually really want always ends up in some form of tension. However, when I allow myself to make 'selfish' decisions, I clearly see that the outcome is usually beneficial for everyone involved."*

Constantly remind yourself to reflect on whether your own desires drive you or if you're simply fulfilling someone else's expectations.

This is where being selfish is correct for you.

## Ego Projected Authority

This is one of the rarest forms of Authorities, which means it is natural that you feel different from the rest of humanity. You are a Projector, so you already know you need to wait for the recognition and invitations, but with your decision-making, especially around what invitations to accept, your limits have to be tested! You have a powerful sense of will, but you need to feel a sense of excitement to know your decision is truly correct for you. You are here to go beyond yourself and others, and whatever you do must always fuel this spirit inside you. If you do not feel it - it is a NO for you.

A lot in your life will depend on the correctness of the people around you. People define your life path- who you live and work with and who you spend your time with. These people must allow you to be your absolute self. Be mindful of other people's expectations of you, and don't let them define you.

Everything you do every day has to have a sense of excitement for you in it, as if they are taking you closer to a distant goal. Every decision in your life leads to a bigger decision. If you are bored with your life, business, or marketing, you have made some small incorrect decision or a compromise, and you will have to wait until true recognition finds you. While you are waiting for recognition in your business, create content around the things that excite you! Waiting is not a passive state of doing nothing.

I worked with an Ego Projected Projector client last year and had an incredible opportunity to observe these mechanics firsthand. This powerful female entrepreneur already built a huge company when her heart was in it, even though, as a Projector, she is a non-energy Type, and yet she was sporting so many accomplishments and was already truly successful. She felt to me more like a Manifesting Generator. I could feel that power when she spoke about what she truly felt excited about and her mission. The content she created in that zone was powerfully compelling, and it attracted clients to her business.

But when she faced marketing tactics she thought she "should" use - perhaps because her celebrity business mentor insisted that she should take that route - she was facing complete creative emptiness and confusion. Her heart was not in it. It was not exciting for her, and so she had no access to her willpower. It caused exhaustion, apathy, and the need to step back to rediscover that drive within.

Here is again a great lesson not to let others condition your decisions!

## Volitional Authorities Summary

***Trust your heart!***

***When you are true to yourself, you will make the most aligned and correct decisions. Don't let the presence of others affect you, no matter what they may think or say or if they consider you arrogant or obnoxious. Always follow your heart.***

# Chapter Fifteen

# Vocal Authority Group

## Speak Your Truth

This is another minority group in the realm of decision-making Authorities. And although this is, again, not a mainstream approach, I agree with Rudd's decision to group them all together. At the end of the day, all of the Authorities in this group use their voice to come to or channel the correct decision.

If you belong to this Authority group, your Design has a lot of openness. Your chart may say Self-Projected Authority, Environmental, Mental, or No Authority. An issue with so much openness and decision-making comes from a lack of definition to guide your body or excitement, like in previous cases.

You also are highly affected by other people's presence, whose chemistry can be overpowering and can affect making decisions easily. The certainty you feel with someone - even when they do not discuss anything with you - can dissipate when you are alone again, leaving you even more confused and uncertain.

This is why you need to know how to "deal" with your specific decision-making in a way that brings you to the correct one.

## Self-Projected Authority

This Authority is specific to Projectors with a lot of openness and G-Centre defined. As a Projector, you already know that crucial decisions in your life always come out of very specific invitations, where recognition for who you are is a must. So, you have to focus on waiting to be recognised in order for these invitations to come into your life, and then have a reliable technique to ensure you are accepting a correct - for you - invitation.

Your Human Design has a "secret" way of making sure that your decisions can be made easily and without stressing about them. And it is so simple - you just need a "sounding board" to talk AT (not to ask for their opinion) - and watch how you feel while you are talking through it out loud. Your voice is literally channelling your Higher Self.

This is a purely mechanical Authority. Only when you talk about something out loud will you get to know what you actually want. It comes right from your soul, not emotions or mental reasoning. The moment the correct decision comes out of you through your voice, you will feel it and have to trust in it. Sometimes you may be genuinely surprised by your decisions. The challenge you face here is not to try to explain or reason why you are making this decision. It is YOUR TRUTH, your Higher Self guidance, and you do not have to justify it to others or even yourself. This requires practice and surrendering to this guidance completely. It will help to experiment with letting it be your "driver" and to watch what happens. If your Mind gets too loud or anxious, you can note what it says but lovingly ignore it. With time this will become easier and easier.

Another important key for you is to have a lot of space from other people to get to that point of clarity about your decisions. Make sure your "sounding boards" are good listeners and do not disturb you or upset you in any way. Neither should they be the type of people ready to "give you advice" - it is the opposite of the role you need your confidants to play.

## Wait & Discuss: Environmental Authority / No Authority

This does not mean anything bad! It just means your decision-making process is very different. Your secret is not to rush it but to allow much more TIME for this process. You cannot be pushed or pressured, or you will end up paying for it. Usually, people with Environmental Authority are Mental Projectors who do not have Inner Authority and therefore rely on being in the correct environment and trusted advisors to use as sounding boards.

My daughter, Chantelle, is a Mental Projector with Environmental Authority in her design, with only two centres (Head and Ajna) defined. This means she thinks a lot, but as a Mental Projector, her Mind should never be relied on in making decisions; it is just too loud and anxious. As a Mental Projector, one has no reliable way to "KNOW' in their body either. I see how Chantelle always floats between a "yes" and a "no," and she generally needs much more time to decide on anything, not to mention the mental anxiety it causes.

Yet the secret is simple- allow it time and discuss. While you are waiting for the clarity to naturally occur (so you are trusting it and trying your best not to be anxious about "knowing"), you can do whatever research you need meanwhile. Ask for second opinions, get trials, and ensure return/refund policies are in place. The "sounding board" technique will also work for you, but remember that it will take more than one person (as you can easily get conditioned by that person's chemistry). You should have a "collection" of three or more people you can talk to while waiting for your clarity to arrive. Just relax and trust that time will serve what is most aligned and correct for you.

Those with No Authority (Reflectors) get conditioned not just by other people but even more by planetary transits, especially the Moon, which activates different energies throughout the 28-day lunar cycle. This means that it takes a while for you to feel the decision through all the various activations. As you go through these activations, you can experience a sudden knowing (often reported by Reflectors).

This always makes me think of my first marriage to a Reflector. We were young and bold, and we decided to get married two weeks into dating. This decision created a huge conflict with my fiancé's mom, which was rightfully completely against this madness. She created so much drama that I asked my fiancé to withdraw our marriage application from the registry office. That couldn't be worse than all of that stress and conflict, especially for my completely open Emotional centre. However, just a week before the date we were supposed to get married, my fiancé turned around to me and asked, *"Well, are you going to marry me on Saturday, or what?"*

Somehow, he intuitively felt he needed time to make his own decision, and it took him almost a full lunar cycle to feel through it, and then he knew. That marriage, although just three years short, was fundamental for our life stories, helping us emigrate and create Chantelle. My first Reflector husband held space for my dreams and helped me make some of them happen because he entered this marriage correctly. I - on the other hand- did not! It was me who proposed, so I initiated completely against my Projector strategy and not following my Spleen but more my Mind, which was getting tired of the constant search for my other half. Plus, he was incredibly gorgeous - I could not resist! But he was not "The One" I was looking for.

Another wonderful point Rudd is making about No Authority people is that while they need time to make decisions about themselves, they often have the ability to see what is right or wrong for other people almost immediately. This is a powerful gift, especially if you are in the business of coaching, consulting, or advising. Trust that you have the aura to attract people who truly want your advice and can be helped through it.

## Vocal Group summary

***Trust your voice and allow some time for clarity to emerge.***

***Make sure your trusted "sounding boards" are allowing you to come to your decisions on your own in order to have ease with this process.***

# Part Four

*Profile Lines and Their Marketing Archetypes*

# Chapter Sixteen

# *Your Brand Identity*

## The Key To Showing Up Authentically

I am most excited about this section, and now we are talking about the most practical application of Human design for marketing, in my option and expertise. All juicy details are very attractive to our Minds, but they can also be a distraction from taking action. Profile lines are where we can truly understand the natural way for us to express ourselves and also how others perceive us and connect to us. That is what marketing is in a nutshell - building an emotional connection between a product and a buyer. You can embrace it and lean into your natural traits or angles you can take when expressing yourself through your content.

Content is King, they say - and understanding our brand personality expressed through our Human Design Profiles is how we can show up in our full royal selves - and attract the best clients while we are at it!

Your Profile shows how you are designed when you ARE YOURSELF. At the same time, it shows how others see and perceive you. It may not be so apparent to you until you become aware of it. You can then make that frequency even more magnetic to draw in the right people.

What does it tell you? It will give you permission to be an introverted loner if that is where you are at your happiest. Or it will remove the need to create a "me, me, me" show and focus your energy entirely on building your network. No self-shaming.

It will help you identify your specific type of wisdom. Is it about long-term visions? Is it about practical solutions at hand? Is it about the deep understanding of the core that offers security? Is it allowing others to feel safe when they make mistakes? Or is it just about you getting lost in your own creative process?

When you know what your Profile identifies, you can build your offers, content, and marketing strategies around the magnetism of that specific energy. You can use specific words that identify it in your copy, define your unique selling point, and so much more.

The conviction this gives your brand voice is incredible because you are not trying to be something that is not natural to YOU. You embody your authenticity, and that pulls in the right people as if by magic.

Unlike some of the Human Design coaches who base their Marketing Archetypes on your energy type, I am very opposed to that approach. Too much surface-level advice tries to merge the information with some practical application without a deeper understanding or even having previous experience with messaging or marketing businesses to see what works and what truly does not work. Even without Human Design flavour, the marketing coaching industry is full of nonsense strategies, sold purely because there is a demand for "templates" and "tell me what to do." This is what caused my complete burnout with being part of that world before I leaned into my own Human Design.

My goal is to marry the awareness about specific energies and how we perceive ourselves and others with the marketing strategies, and especially developing a brand voice that allows building aligned and mutually transformational relationships. This is what marketing is all about - relationships. When it comes to Human Design, in order to understand how we build relationships, we need to go deeper than just aura interactions. Your Type is how you engage with the world. Your Profile is your personality traits and how you express yourself and engage with others.

I developed my Marketing Archetypes based on our Human Design Profile Lines - they are determined by the decimal numbers after the Personality and Design Sun gates in your chart. As the Sun is the closest star, its influence is the strongest in determining our personality and how we are seen by and interact with others in many ways.

I have done a lot of research to find the best analogy to illustrate the roles each line is representing, which makes it easier to understand and practically use this awareness in the way we are showing up. Everyone knows who they are deep inside, but often we deny ourselves the right to be ourselves because we get conditioned to believe things "should" be done a certain way.

Awareness about your "role" will only validate what you already know deep inside. But with that confirmation, you can empower yourself to trust and rely on this role to make your visibility magnetic and infuse your brand voice with conviction that compels your ideal clients to stop the scroll, pay attention, and raise their hands, eager to work with you.

Of all the different interpretations, I find the original Ra Uru Hu's illustration of people in a house the most accurate. It provides the best understanding of what and how these roles show themselves. This is such juicy information, and I go so much deeper into it inside my Marketing Blueprint By Design™ reports. But in this book, I want to give you a bottom-line summary of each archetype that can help you embrace your authentic voice - even if we never worked together.

# Chapter Seventeen

# Line 1: Investigator

## Your Marketing Archetype: The Maven

In Human Design, Line 1 is called The Investigator. It is a person whose mind needs to know that the essence, the foundation of everything they come across, is solid, secure, and safe. Therefore, they are someone who is driven to make sure they attain that security in their lives. In Ra's illustration of the house, a line 1 person is down in the basement, inspecting the foundation for possible cracks or instabilities.

It is a very intellectual line, as it will make the person jump into so many "rabbit holes" in order to get a firm grasp of everything they research. And it is fair to mention that although a line 1 person is focused on the details, knowing everything about the subject is not always what motivates them. It is only that essence that, when it feels concrete, creates a very solid and unique perspective on the whole subject. They need to know "the bottom line."

Over their lives, people with line 1 jump into a vast number of different areas of interest, and they end up building quite an array of skills and mastering many trades. This makes each line 1 person a treasure trove of creative skills. Plus, they gain so much knowledge through constant investigation and processing of this information. They have an ability to "see through the fluff" and know the real deal from the "industry nonsense". This gives them a lot of authority and adds trustworthiness when they share what they see.

This is why I call this Marketing Archetype - The Maven. This is a person with a profound understanding and authority on a niche or a range of subjects. This is where positioning yourself as an Authority is key for a 1st line person. Think about first impressions. How can your online presence, starting from your visuals, immediately place you as someone who knows what they are talking about? The best way to achieve that is by leveraging publicity. You can focus on getting into larger industry publications as a guest contributor or a feature. You can speak on industry podcasts and land a media feature on a TV network. It is all attainable, and with your unique perspective, backed with such profound research, they will be happy to have you.

Yet the one thing that can stop you- and here we are discussing an Archetype shadow - is your Impostor Syndrome. You might feel like you are never ready to share and that you need to research more and more. You can get stuck in jumping between rabbit holes without actually creating any visibility at all. All because you might feel that you do not know "enough," and someone will definitely call you out on it (the mothership of Impostor Syndrome fears).

My conscious line is line 1 (I am a 1/3 profile person), and so I know that issue painfully well. In fact, I am always feeling inadequate, not enough, "not an expert," and like I am winging it. Even RIGHT NOW, as I am writing this, there is this little voice in my head trying to tell me I should not be claiming authority on this subject. At the end of the day, I have not got any official Human Design certifications to "prove" I know what I know.

And yet, I personally care very little about certifications, simply because traditional education is based on the "scope" of things and not their essence. So, looking back at my academic years studying marketing, there is nothing that it brought to the table in practical terms. I had to discover, learn, research, and make up my own mind about everything I know or do in my business. Line 1 is not about a certification to prove you know what you know. It is about getting a firm grasp on understanding what you need to feel secure and solid in this knowledge.

In your content, if you have line 1, you can confidently lean into your Thought-Leader positioning. In fact, having a strong online presence (both visual and content-wise) will only strengthen your self-recognition as an authority. So, build that shiny cover and use the angle "*This is what I see*" to unlock your brand voice magnetism. It is ok for you to talk about your perspectives and findings, and it is absolutely fine for you to talk about yourself a lot - especially if you are a 1/3 profile.

Through your introspective sharing, you get to save people in your world so much time and effort trying to find the core and figure out what is worth focusing on and what is just a smoke screen. This is what you do - and your voice can be trusted.

Just be careful not to overload people with details. We, line 1s, tend to get heavy sometimes. We have this rock, slower-moving, slower-paced energy - so try to express yourself without massively long detail. I know you won't be able to do that in one-liners.

My Facebook posts are super long, and I cannot even consider LinkedIn because of their character limit, but I always try to read back and edit out what is not essential. In my podcast interviews, I like having a few bullet points and having some prep done on the topic, so I know I do not go off on a 2-hour monologue and lose my listener.

## Line 1 summary:

Your brand personality is a **leading authority in your niche.** Prioritise building a shiny cover presenting you as a thought leader and an authority in your niche. Share **what you see** and **have discovered from your unique perspective**. When feeling the impostor syndrome, focus on sharing what you are solid in knowing and allow yourself to build on that as you go. Do not hold back because you do not feel you are 'enough" as an expert. You are probably at a ninja level already without even realising it.

As a leading authority, deeply understanding your subject matter is essential in building trust with your audience. Cultivate your curiosity and continuously expand your knowledge to stay ahead of the curve. Share personal perspectives and expert insights that are relevant and valuable to your target audience.

When creating content, simplify complex concepts and use language that connects with your audience. Q&A sessions will help you demonstrate your expertise further and strengthen your position as a respected authority in your field.

# Chapter Eighteen

# Line 2: Hermit

## Your Marketing Archetype: The Natural

In Human Design, Line 2 is often referred to as "The Hermit." People with this line have an innate need for solitude and personal space to indulge in activities they truly love. This precious alone time holds the key to unlocking their unique gift - something they are designed to experience in their lifetime. I like to call the Line 2 archetype "The Natural" because these people so effortlessly express their talents without even trying or following a step-by-step approach.

However, there can be a struggle for people with Line 2 to articulate their exceptional abilities or explain the methods behind their success. Traditional marketing methods may feel challenging and uncomfortable for them. As a result, they may hesitate to "put themselves out there," especially as they thrive in solitude. This difficulty in pinpointing their gifts and effectively communicating them can sometimes lead to feelings of insecurity - a common trait among Line 2 people.

Let me share an intriguing observation with you. One of my favourite messaging experts, Eleanore Strong, whom I deeply admire, excels at illustrating messaging mistakes and providing examples of how to avoid them in her content. I was genuinely surprised to discover that Line 2 is her primary personality line (Eleanore is a 2/4 Sacral Generator). She seems to so effortlessly "explain" how to write compelling content to attract high-end clients.

However, during our private conversation, Eleanore confessed that she herself only became clear on how she achieved it a few months before our chat. I had been following her for years at that point, and it was a fascinating fact. Just like with all natural talents, we often struggle to break down and pinpoint what exactly makes it so good. Eleanor didn't seem to have internal clarity around her gift for quite a while, even though all that time, her writing exuded confidence and strength. She now positions her client attraction system as the "Strong Method." I highly recommend following Eleanore for messaging advice.

One more very interesting note: Eleanore's breakthrough didn't happen overnight. It took her nearly seven years to discover that sweet spot where her system started generating consistent and substantial profits. This perfectly aligns with the nature of Line 2. Sometimes, a 2nd line person literally stumbles upon something that helps unleash their gift, something that resonates so much, and it becomes second nature almost overnight. But while the mastery itself may occur relatively quickly, the search for that gift can be a long and winding journey.

If you haven't discovered your unique gift yet, it's crucial to focus on what genuinely captivates you and create uninterrupted space to dive into it. Remember that, just like anything natural, your gift may not appear extraordinary to you, and you may not fully grasp its value. Let's use the metaphor of a house to illustrate this point. Imagine someone performing something incredible in a room on the ground floor with open curtains. People outside observe and yearn to be part of the action, calling out, "*This is brilliant! Show us more! Share it with us, please!*"

Even if you are not a Projector by design, Line 2 represents a "projected" line. The beauty lies in the fact that those who appreciate your unique gifts will naturally seek you out when the time is right. It's as if Line 2 loves being in solitude, fully immersed in their natural talents, while the rest of us watch in awe and desire to witness more. In terms of profile combinations, for those with a 2/4 profile, your social network becomes a crucial puzzle piece, attracting the right connections. For those with a 2/5 profile, the seductive and magnetic energy of Line 5 draws external attention and fascination beyond the immediate network.

Let's talk about that "call". When people call you out, you have the opportunity to share your mastered gifts with them, allowing them to benefit from your natural talents and reward you in return. But you don't need to push for attention. People naturally gravitate toward you. And if their "call" resonates with your Strategy and Authority, it indicates the right timing and alignment.

There is one exception to Line 2 people, and that is the 5/2 profile. In this case, the mechanics are slightly different. While any other Line 2 individual may simply do something and have others point out how good it is, making them aware of their gift, for those with a 5/2 profile, it is only when you yourself recognise your gift that you can respond to the calls of others. Because, no matter what others see in you, if you don't see it yourself, their feedback will be nothing but noise to you. Stubbornness is also one of the attributes associated with Line 2.

Lastly, it is vital for any Line 2 person to understand their relationships with others. Line 2 tends to be somewhat of a perfectionist when it comes to other people, and if a relationship is anything less than perfect, it can result in deep disappointment internally. At the lowest frequency, this disappointment can even lead to serious negative projections onto others, where the issue may be nothing more than a lack of harmony. This is one aspect of the Projection Field that we will focus on when we discuss Line 5 individuals later in this book.

Again, this is why following your Strategy and Authority to decide who you should allow into your world and who is incorrect is vital for Line 2. Imperfect relationships will trigger your need to retreat and escape from visibility. Remember, you can't really be called out if nobody sees you. By being more discerning with the people in your life, you will also grant yourself the freedom to show up when you feel like it and be alone and do your thing when you need to. In terms of content, it's all about moving away from seeking validation from others and instead focusing on demonstrating your talent through writing about your experiences and thought processes or showcasing what you do if it applies.

## Line 2 summary:

You need to "**become your own muse**" and lean into what draws you in rather than what you think "they" want to hear. **Your brand personality is a natural genius.**

As a natural genius, finding the easiest and most comfortable way to share your knowledge is key. Embrace your unique approach to sharing information in your work, blog posts, live streams, and other content. Though you may be introverted at times, make the most of opportunities to express yourself.

People will be drawn to your brilliance and seek out your insights. Share content that demonstrates you in action or your thought processes and highlights the insightful, revelatory moments that stem from the mastery of your subject matter.

# Chapter Nineteen

# Line 3: Martyr (Experiential)

## Your Marketing Archetype: The Pathfinder

In Human Design, this line is called The Martyr. It's a strange and unpleasant word, but it is fitting because line 3 always looks to improve and innovate, and so its life is a constant series of trials and failures, again and again, before it discovers that thing that works.

It doesn't sound easy, and it is not. This is the only line that is "of a material plane" by its nature - basically, they are the only ones who live in "the real world." While line 1 is here to look for cracks in foundations and line 2 is here to focus on their gifts, line 3 is here to test what is not working - and tell others. When you hear that all good things come through hard work, that is likely what a 3rd line person once said. Failure does not exist for such people. They fail, get back on their feet, adjust their course, and try again. And often, they keep trying and trying until they find something that DOES work - resulting in a lot of material benefits. This is the "money" line, but the magic here is in not giving up trying.

Everyone in my family has line 3 in their profiles. In fact, they are all 3/5 profile people. I think it is something karmic for me to experience this specific profile - that is, testing my line 1's need for security and solid foundations almost on a daily basis. It is so ironic to me to talk about line 3 being innovative because one of the biggest conflicts with my 3/5 mom in my life was over her coming to Ireland to help with my baby and completely ruining all the routines I had established.

I had been told I had a "golden child," a "textbook" child. I established routines other mothers would only dream of. My daughter did not need to be rocked to sleep at night or during daily naps. She just fell asleep (and slept all night through from the age of 2 months). Why? I had some set ways to do things, and through these systems, I was able to build habits that helped this baby follow very peaceful daily routines.

But when my mom moved in, she started "breaking the rules." It was impossible to rely on or expect that what I specifically asked for would be followed through according to plan. Within six months, all my routines were destroyed, and new ways (that I did not agree with) were established. I love my mom dearly, and I took the backseat then. I knew if I pushed, it would result in a conflict. She just couldn't follow the rulebook. She HAD to find "better" ways. In her opinion, of course...

The same thing happened with my husband Les, who was also a 3/5. No matter what I asked him to do, he always did it somewhat (if not completely) differently. And he got quite annoyed when I confronted him about it - of course- because line 3 is all about experimenting with finding the better way to do things. Faster. Cheaper. More efficiently. Just the idea of trying something new seems exciting to them.

Of course, all the trials and failures do not just roll off line 3 person's back. There is criticism and even more powerful self-criticism that develops through their lifetime of constant mistakes and errors. And therefore, they can hold back - to avoid being criticised. And I see it often in their marketing and business too. They can get stuck on trying to learn or understand something without trying it confidently (and being confident that they will get it wrong a lot at the start) - which is the opposite of what they are designed to be.

My marketing archetype for line 3 is the Pathfinder. A robotic explorer on a distant planet that looks for ways to access and collect data to send it back to Earth. In its explorations, it often falls and has to realign to gain a vertical position. There is a chance that it will fail. There is a chance that it will break and get stuck there forever. But that is not the point.

The point is that it is looking for a reliable path that others can confidently walk on later. As the 3rd line, this is what your content should be all about. Your stories of trying and testing various things; your discoveries of what is not working, not safe, or not what it seems; sharing what direction is unreliable; and through these stories, you unlock such powerful and relatable magnetism. You are literally telling others that they cannot fail with you as an example of resilience and persistence on your journey to success...and beyond.

## Line 3 Summary:

Your brand personality is a **Resilient Innovator.** You embody the essence of what it means to be human. Imperfect but wonderful. By **sharing your raw and authentic experiences**, you inspire and expand the perspectives of others.

Your unwavering commitment to self-discovery and growth attracts others to follow your journey every step of the way. Maintain your curious spirit as you continue to transform and grow. Your resilience and positive storytelling exude confidence and inspire others to do the same.

To create content that showcases your Line 3 storytelling, share personal stories that highlight your journey, including both your triumphs and challenges. Talk about how it all started and the transformations you've experienced along the way. Create content about what is not working and how you are exploring ways to improve it and make it more effective and efficient. Use humour - as it is your go-to tool to surviving such a bumpy ride in the first place.

# Chapter Twenty

# Line 4: Opportunist

## Your Marketing Archetype: The Influencer

I love line 4 people, maybe because when you get to know them, they are the most friendly and loyal people. Their relationships with people in their world are the key factor in their lives, and this determines how they can achieve success in business and marketing. **Spoiler alert - by NOT using traditional, modern digital marketing strategies.**

These guys are more old school - remember the world before the internet? Even before print media altogether? I bet you don't - but the fact that businesses have existed for thousands of years means there is one reliable way to build a business without relying on the mercy of strangers, right?

Up until about 70 years before now, any traditional business owner knew that in order to survive, they must focus on their connections and existing clients for return business and referrals. It is so easy to frown on getting business by referrals today (it feels that attracting clients online is so easy, according to the online marketing gurus out there who promote a "post it and they will come" mentality. But the reality is that it is not an effective strategy- no matter what your energies are), and it is definitely an exhausting strategy for anyone with line 4 in their profile. Unfortunately, their trusting nature often means they put their trust in the wrong people. This is why following your strategy and authority is such key.

In Human Design, line 4 is called the Opportunist. This is the first line of the upper trigram - which means this is the first line where karmically people play a more important role (the first three lines are focused within to learn karmic lessons about themselves). Line 4 is the first one that raises its head and looks over to "the other side" people out there. And here lies the gift of any line 4 person: they are born to build strong and deep relationships. It is something that comes naturally to them (even if you are a 2/4 person, and like your "hermit" time, you are so natural at building and maintaining your relationships and social life). In the house illustration, line 4 is having a house party, and you can see them mingling in the room filled with their friends and family.

The most important aspect to understand when it comes to marketing your business and your online visibility is that, as a line 4, your influence will always be on people who know you. They are the only ones who feel your heart's warmth and get how much you care. Strangers tend not to "see" you and your gifts. They need to first get to know you a little. Ideally, they need to be introduced into your network through existing members of that network. This is why in marketing, your network is your golden mile - not just because of direct sales and opportunities, but also as a way to expand your network with more correct people.

Building communities where you can show up - not as a teacher, but as a connector and networker, to be the glue that holds it together could be highly beneficial for you. If you follow your Strategy and Authority to re-align with what you do and trust your own truth (and not showing up in a way you assume will help to be "liked" by others, which can be your not-Self-expression), the business will flourish.

The quality of your network is crucial, not just to your business success but even to your personal well-being. Complete strangers are not just wrong but can be detrimental, as their energy can bring a subtle but very negative effect on your network, as well as the opportunities arising from it, and essentially your influence within it. When I create Marketing Blueprint By Design™ reports for my line 4 clients, we go deep into how the four key themes of Connection, Network, Opportunity and Influence play out in real life and marketing. You can order it at

The bottom line is that your most aligned opportunities will come when people who join your network come from someone that is already part of it. Referral marketing and affiliate marketing (offering your network to promote your offers for a commission) are great ways to extend your reach.

One more vital note about line 4 is that although networking is your "jam," you need periods of retreat to recharge, so do not feel bad when you are feeling withdrawn. Always factor in some "valleys" as you are conquering your "mountains" and enjoy that time alone.

## Line 4 summary:

Your brand personality is a **friendly influencer.** You are here to develop and grow your influence through your network. You need to be "one of them" to be their leader. But don't try to "be nice to be liked". Stay true to your opinions and stances. If things get too much, take time to recharge alone when needed.

Your nature and passion for sharing your knowledge and experience make you a natural leader. When part of your network, your audience is attentive and receptive to your message, making you an effective influencer.

Make the most of opportunities to collaborate and build relationships with others in your field. Use your strong connection with your audience to share content that resonates on a personal level, helping them to become more aware of their own challenges and opportunities for growth.

# Chapter Twenty-One

# *Line 5: Heretic*

## Your Marketing Archetype: The Solutionist

A complete opposite to line 4, line 5 people's influence does not work on people around them as well. In fact, line 5 is here to attract and influence strangers. And not just that, you are here to influence strangers in a moment of their crisis.

Line 5 in Human Design is called The Heretic and represents the "Will" or the drive to take action and make things happen. People with a Line 5 in their Human Design chart are known for their determination and ability to manifest their goals and desires. They have strong willpower and are able to push through obstacles to achieve their objectives. They are also often leaders and decision-makers, able to take charge and direct others in achieving a common goal.

What line 5 person needs to be very aware of is that from the moment they are born, they are designed to deal with the Projection Field. People - especially in close circles, like family and friends, will project their hopes and aspirations on a line 5 person, and if those are not met, there is a distinct "switch" that can happen. When this happens, the projection turns negative, as now they are projecting their disappointment.

However, it is important to note that there are always positive projections before there are negative projections. This is the mechanics of the 5th line. When we meet a line 5 purpose, our first impression is that this person CAN - it is a positive projection. And when they cannot or do not, then there is a switch to negative projection, often a very powerful one. Those negative projections are highly unpleasant and hard to deal with.

There is a lot of "drama" in line 5 people's line, so the understanding that all that drama is about the people who are projecting their own feelings can be quite liberating. Of course, this requires a level of awareness and also knowing the right timing to speak and act, especially when it has to do with offering solutions or "fixing" others. Timing and practicality are the keys to unlocking the alignment and living in their purpose without drama.

The key thing in terms of business solutions and marketing them is to understand that people only come to line 5 in times of crisis. In the house analogy, the line 5 person is seen in the window on the upper floor, through the closed curtains (so we do not see them clearly). But they look so magnetic like they have the key, the secret to all our problems. They look like they naturally can come down and save us from our crisis. And truly, a line 5 person has the gift of seeing through the mess and finding an extremely practical solution. However, **when there is no crisis, anything line 5 does or says pretty much "falls on deaf ears."**

Based on this observation, it becomes very clear why "pain point marketing" is where line 5 will be the most magnetic. Let's look at it closer. When you act with integrity, which I am sure you do, "pain point marketing" is not only correct but aligned with the way people respond to you. Do not get put off by the terminology - think about the fact that it is only in crisis when people "summon you as their General". If there is no crisis, they do not "need" you - so your marketing goes over their heads.

Of all lines in Human Design, line 5, the Heretic, is here to point directly at the problems and offer applicable solutions - which is essentially what "pain point" marketing is. It does not need to be manipulative either, unlike a lot of people, especially in the field of spirituality, tend to assume. When I am not happy with something to the point of wanting to change it, and even more important to the point of being happy to pay to change it - this is my "pain point." And this is when, of all other lines, I will be drawn to hire you - because your solutions make perfect sense and give me hope.

The biggest issue I observe with all my line 5 clients, and there are plenty as they are my fractals, is that they are unwilling to tap into their true "heretic" nature and speak more confidently about the issues they see. They are trying to stay very generic, very top level, or they talk about something that is not relevant to NOW, to HERE, to the actual PAIN their potential clients are in. In other words, they are not using the most magnetic part and not embodying their seductive quality of leadership in crisis. Instead, they are trying to stay safe from the projections - and getting nowhere as a result. Until they gain awareness of these mechanics and start showing up so boldly – their whole world opens up for success.

## Line 5 summary:

Your brand personality is **an inspiring leader [in crisis].** Your message has the power to reach and impact many souls.

When in crisis, people are drawn to you for your ability to provide practical solutions to their problems. Without a crisis, your influence goes over their heads, so try not to stay too safe or too generic. Use your strategic thinking and authoritative voice to help others. Hone in on the painful issues or challenges they experience.

Maintain strong boundaries to ensure you can serve your audience effectively. Focus on building an attractive, polished-looking powerful brand, and set clear and strong guidelines on what you CAN and CANNOT deliver to manage the projections. Base those promises on what is most practical and doable for you. Be careful about the timing of your actions, as it can directly affect your reputation.

# Chapter Twenty-Two

# Line 6: Role Model

## Your Marketing Archetype: The Tribe's Elder

Line 6, called The Role Model, is very, very special.

In fact, people with line 6 are beings of the new era. It is where everything below in the 6-line hexagram combusts into something new. Look at it from the point of karmic influence. Lines 1, 2, and 3 are here to learn something about themselves. Their life journey is focused on their personal karmic lessons. Line 4 is the first line that even considers "the other" in their lives, yet it is still all evolving around learning about themselves in relation to the other. It is only line 5 that is openly focused on others and dealing with others' projections at all times. This is the only line that conditions others - telling them what is right and what is wrong and offering them solutions to their problems.

But when it comes to line 6, we are entering something completely new. The focus turns back inwards. Line 6 is here to experience themselves in the most perfect form. And as they achieve this perfection in being themselves, they karmically affect everyone else around them on a personal level. They then become a Role Model to others, pumping their very unique, new tri-partial life structure into the world around them. Let's have a look at that first.

Line 6 person's development has three very distinct stages of maturity.

From birth to around 27 years (their Saturn return), they live like line 3- which means experiencing the material side of life, making mistakes, and bumping into life quite literally. And while line 3 people have a natural resilience to shake off the "dirt" and start again, line 6 people do not, so they can feel pretty disempowered and discouraged in this phase. Then they go into the second part, which lasts till their Chiron return at around 50-51 years old. This is where they retreat and reflect on their experiences. It is a calmer stage, but they may prefer to observe rather than participate. This is why this stage is often referred to in Human Design as being "on the roof". In the house metaphor, line 6 person is literally sitting on the roof and looking at the horizon.

It is only after their Chiron return at the age of 50/51 that the line 6 person has processed their experiences and becomes mature to truly step into the karmic role of "The Role Model" or the Tribe Elder, as I call my line 6 marketing archetype. The wisdom they develop about achieving that perfection in who they are is so profound, and it is contagious. As line 6, your life's most influential time is going to be after you reach your 50s. And as there are so many Generators in the world with line 6 in their profile, they pump this energy through their open porous aura and "affect" or condition others around.

I do not know about you, but as I am approaching my 47th birthday, I do not even think I started my life's most prominent part. I definitely feel that the modern world is not about "making it in your 20s" but much more about waking up to what you can do in your 50s and beyond, and it is beautiful. Imagine all of the experience and maturity, as well as knowing who you are, that you have gathered before you are 50. How much more powerful this influence and wisdom is compared to when one is in their 20s or 30s. It is breathtaking, and we have all those line 6 people around to thank for this gift! This is how their influence is karmic. This is how they condition others, not by telling them what to do, but by being themselves in the highest consciousness, the perfection of who they are.

Line 6s are pretty amazing even before they reach their 50s. I have met so many line 6 people who are just wise beyond their years, but of course, some extra real-life experience is needed sometimes to truly solidify this wisdom. This is what the tri-partial life structure is needed for.

And so, when it comes to marketing, line 6 has the vision. It is as if their eye is on the horizon. They are the ones that see the bigger picture. They are the ones that can teach us to see the bird's eye view and understand that it is so crucial - especially as all other lines are so focused on themselves or solving practical problems we often lose sight of that bigger picture.

The only thing I must mention is that when one is focusing on the horizon too much, it is easy to become vague and unclear, so structures are essential and extremely helpful for anyone with a line 6 profile. I remember loving how Robin Winn MFT, the author of "Understanding Your Clients Through Human Design" and a 6/2 Generator had a brilliant layout in her book, where she would offer a summary, then bullet point of what she would cover, and then focus on each of those bullet points. Maybe this was not a natural way for her to organize the book, and he had a coach helping her out with this structure, but it helps consume and really understand what she is teaching in the book so well.

I sometimes meet some 6/2 people who struggle so much to express what they are about simply because they are not using a reliable structure to organise their thoughts. If you have line 6 in your profile and lean into structuring your thoughts and ideas, you will find it will unlock your creativity, create really great programs you can offer, and attract so many more clients to your business.

I also suggest you focus on storytelling in your marketing. Show them who you are. Make it about your processes, lifestyle, and visions. This is where your role model magnetism is. Just by being YOU, you inspire people to want to grow and be more like you.

## Line 6 summary:

Your brand personality is a **Transformative Role Model**, and your essence exudes wisdom and foresight. Your innate ability to see things before they happen sets you apart. Embrace your authentic self and trust your vision as you embark on a journey of turning life experience into wisdom.

Your marketing strategy should emphasise your experience and expertise, positioning you as a trusted expert in your field. Share structured, actionable tips and guidance, drawing on your wisdom and personal journey to help others transform their lives. Let authenticity be your guiding light, allowing your true self to shine through in your marketing messages.

Use your natural inclination to offer insights, predictions, and trends, leveraging your ability to "see things before they happen." Position yourself as a role model, highlighting the positive impact you've had on others and positioning yourself as a mentor and guide.

# Part Five

## The Juicy Secrets Of Aligned Visibility

# Chapter Twenty-Three

# Expressing Your Uniqueness In Business & Marketing

## Understanding The Basics Of Circuitry

One of the great places for inspiration around the specifics of your influence and choosing the most aligned "containers" to deliver your products and services hides within your circuitry. Let me explain.

Human Design circuitry is a system that helps us understand how we interact and connect with others. Each gate in our chart belongs to a channel, which is part of a stream, a sub-circuit, and ultimately one of the three main circuits: Collective, Tribal or Individual. The channels inside a specific circuitry can be manifested, manifested generated, generated or projected – echoing the strategy of the type with the same name.

These energies have a profound role to play as they receive, transform, and express the themes that will emerge in our lives.

In business, understanding your circuitry can be very helpful. But please remember that the information below is condensed to give you an idea, inspire you, and give you something to "bounce off". There is so much more to it, but you do not need to jump into every

Human Design rabbit hole. Just use this section for your awareness and focus on mastering your Strategy and Authority, which will help you make all the right (for you) decisions in the first place - whether you know about the small details or not. But since the Minds loves juicy information, I want to give you just "the gist of it." Please keep in mind that your most prominent circuitry could be different from the channels you see in your chart as it would calculate all active gates on the circuitry, not just the channels. **I can do that inside your Marketing Blueprint By Design™ report. Please go to marketingbyhumandesign.com to order yours today.**

## Collective Circuitry

(Channels: 63/4, 17/62, 16/48, 18/58, 52/9, 5/15, 7/31, 64/47, 11/56, 53/42, 29/46, 13/33, 41/30, 36/35)

The Collective Circuit in Human Design focused on bettering humanity and supporting its growth and evolution. People with a lot of energy in this circuit share their insights and knowledge for the benefit of society as a whole. It serves as a conduit for both "reflection" and "projection" and traverses through three essential awareness centres: the Spleen, Emotional Solar Plexus, and Ajna. Within this intricate circuit, we encounter two minor circuits:

The Understanding Circuit has the power to project patterns into the future, allowing us to step into leadership roles with clarity and purpose. This circuit follows a linear process, focusing on discerning patterns that will shape our future.

The Sensing Circuit invites us to reflect on the past, drawing upon abstract energy to gain wisdom and insights. It operates cyclically, offering us an expansive inward journey of introspection and retrospection.

This beautiful energy of the Collective Circuit empowers us to delve into the realms of both the past and future, offering transformative solutions that support the evolution of humanity. It is perfect for sharing our experiences and knowledge, allowing for collective course corrections and growth.

While most of these channels are projected (need to wait for an invitation before taking action), a few exceptions are manifested (need to inform before acting).

If you have a strong presence in the Collective Circuit, you may feel that you have something to share, and it is not confined to your self-empowerment or supporting your network; it is bigger than that. It is inspiring and creates a picture of a better world. Pretty much any niche can be presented through this angle if this is your most prominent Circuitry. You are born to create evergreen content that is aimed at bettering the world, even if your influence is through one reader at a time.

## Tribal Circuitry

(Channels 45/21, 26/44, 40/37, 32/54, 49/19, 50/27, 6/59)

The Tribal Circuit is focused on supporting the community. It revolves around understanding the fundamental needs of the community and what it takes for its members not only to survive but thrive.

When we explore the Tribal Circuit, we dive into the practical aspects of life on the material plane. We consider the emotional well-being, physical necessities, and even the spiritual dimensions that contribute to a balanced community. People with a lot of energy in this circuit tend to create connections and build relationships with others easily.

There are two circuits inside the Tribal: Ego (Tribal) and Defense.

The Ego Circuit has a special significance as it ensures that our community has the necessary resources to function effectively. It's grounded in the practical aspects of life, emphasizing the values, laws, and systems that support the community's growth. It is a very supportive but also sensitive energy. A lot of it is rooted in the bargain principle: I do this for you, and you do this for me. Keep this in mind when creating collaborations or recruiting clients. Make it clear to them what specifically you may expect in return for your contribution - not everyone has Tribal energy, and they may not operate in the same way. This will avoid everyone from feeling disappointed and unappreciated. While most channels within the Ego Circuit are projected (need to wait to be invited before taking action), one exception is channel 45/21, which is a manifested channel (inform and act).

The Defense Circuit holds the responsibility of protecting life and fostering the creation of new experiences. It brings a sense of intimacy and preservation to the community, reminding us of the importance of connection. The Defense channels are generated. You need to wait to respond for this energy to be expressed correctly.

If you have a strong presence in the Tribal Circuitry, you may be best suited to build connections and relationships with others, which can be useful in networking and building a business that has a lot of support touchpoints. These are perfect energies for group coaching or any program that brings together a group of individuals to work on a common goal or topic. You could market yourself by emphasising the benefits of building connections and relationships with others, such as support and accountability.

## Individual Circuitry

(Channels 61/24, 43/23, 20/57, 12/22, 8/1, 2/14, 28/38, 55/39, 3/60, 10/34, 25/51)

The Individual Circuit embodies the essence of individuality and empowerment. It is a dynamic and transformative energy that awakens when one embraces their unique being. This circuit holds the power of self-empowerment, not only benefiting the individual but also radiating its empowering influence to the collective. It emphasizes that expressing one's individual energy does not come with a guarantee of benefiting the Community or the Collective. Rather, it encourages individuals to authentically express themselves, embracing their true nature without seeking external validation.

Within the Individual Circuit, there are two minor circuits that add depth and dimension.

The Knowing Circuit is about creating unique perspectives, experiences, and patterns through the awareness centres.

The Centering Circuit serves as a guiding force, enabling individuals to find their centre, take proactive steps, and cultivate self-love.

While most channels within this circuit are projected, there are exceptions where energy is either manifested or generated. These variations highlight the diverse ways in which individuality can manifest and thrive in the tapestry of human experience. People with a lot of energy in this circuit tend to care for themselves and ensure their survival.

If you have a strong presence in the Individual Circuit, you may be best suited to create programs that focus on self-empowerment and specific personal practices that perhaps you yourself implement in your life and business. You can create and promote offers and services that help individuals take care of themselves and achieve their personal goals. It may not feel natural for you to share with the world as a whole, so focus your content on yourself- what you do, believe, and use to achieve your goals and dreams. In your marketing, walk your talk and be the inspiration for those who follow you.

## Integration Channels

(20/10, 20/34, 10/57, 57/20)

These channels are a separate circuit group that supports the individual. These four don't really belong to any of the three main groups. They are intimately connected with self-preservation and the empowerment of individual nature, expression, knowledge, direction, identity, and behaviour. They play a vital role in ensuring the Individual's survival and driving the unique mutations necessary for the continued existence and growth of the Community and the Collective.

These channels weave together the intricate tapestry of individuality, allowing for the emergence of charisma, personal power, the pursuit of perfection, and the awakening of higher consciousness. They are catalysts that propel the evolutionary journey of both the individual and the collective. This energy is focused on helping individuals integrate their energy and make the most of their unique design.

The 20/10 and 57/20 are projected channels; they need to wait for an invitation before taking action.

34/57 is generated; it needs something to Respond to.

20/34 is manifesting generated; it needs to wait to respond, leading into instant action and initiation.

If you have a lot of Integration Channels, you may want to focus your marketing efforts on promoting services that help individuals connect with their purpose and find meaning in their lives.

My chart is strongest in the Logical Understanding (37%) and Sensing (22.22%), which belong to the Collective Circuit group, and I also have a strong Knowing circuit (23.9%) which is Individual circuitry. Through the Collective circuit influences, I am here to share the benefits of reliable and repeating patterns for a secure movement into the future and the benefits of past observations and experiences. I have an incredible drive to share what I am discovering, currently through Human Design and marketing, but it was just as important for me to share any time something consumed me- from promoting my music projects to sharing my fashion design obsessions through a dressmaking blog and creating tutorials. It is like I have a need to share it with the world. This is my personal understanding of how the COLLECTIVE circuitry is expressed.

My INDIVIDUAL Knowing Circuit allows me to empower others through mutative experiences (in plain words, by growing and adapting to change). There is a lot of "walking my talk" in my own marketing. I show up and pivot as it is required to find what works for me, my energy levels, my aspirations, and my limits. So many times, my clients tell me how inspired they are watching me adapt and adjust my course.

I have very little TRIBAL circuitry influence, which means I am not that concerned about building tight communities and supporting my Tribe through DOING (supporting, connecting, making agreements or protecting).

In fact, I am indeed a "lone wolf" who loves to share her perspectives and inspire others by example. This creates the magnetism that allows me to build my community, but it does not exist in the form of a tribe or a networking group. Knowing these specifics helps me let go of the "need to build a Tribe' and release the ones I have built before as and when the time comes to move on and grow out of them. In fact, knowing my circuitry helped me build my business, attracting most of my current clients through what I share online - my dominant collective energy- which then gets backed up by how I express myself by focusing on my individual experiences, observations, and discoveries.

By understanding your circuitry, you can gain valuable insights into how you are best designed to support others and cultivate a nourishing business. Indeed, it is not so simple to find out at a glance, and it will take a lot of research to do on your own, so do turn to a professional, like your humble author here, to shorten that journey.

A little note. I am noticing a lot of Human Design advice on specific business models based on circuitry, but I believe this can be misleading. Just because you have this Collective circuitry represented most prominently in your chart does not guarantee that if you decide, for example, to create online courses, they will sell out. So it is not about what specific model you choose. In my opinion, it is about how what you create helps the betterment of the world as a whole. Plus, other aspects of your chart will be even more important in determining how much and which way you want to connect with your clients. This is specifically why what you may see in an Instagram post from a Human Design expert is not what should determine your business model.

# Chapter Twenty-Four

# The Center For Manifestation

## The Misunderstood Throat Center

There is little or no chance of being "discovered" in the noisy online world without showing up and talking about your products and services. And this is why most coaches fail to establish their businesses and give up in the first couple of years.

So HOW can you show up and talk about your value, expertise, and offers in a way that cuts through the noise and attracts the correct people? And how can you do it in a way that FEELS like you are seen, heard & recognised for your excellence as a coach or an expert? (Or just as a great person that you are?)

People are not just born with incredible public speaking skills. These skills can be learned, practised, and mastered over time by anyone ready to dedicate some effort.

In my Human Design, I have Channel 16/48, "The Channel of Wavelength," or the "Design of Talents." But these talents, if we look at talking about what I know with enthusiasm, will only attract the right people if I master my niche and honestly know what I am talking about. My talents are all learned through practice and repetition that are driven by becoming better at whatever it is I am mastering. And that is great news!

This means that becoming good or great – in the case of this topic of being a magnetic speaker – is something ANYONE can achieve. You can work on the tone of your voice, take powerful pauses, and use the speed of talking to create more impact and emotional connection when you tell your stories. And becoming an engaging speaker opens doors to more beautiful invitations and opportunities to establish yourself as an "authority" – claiming your right to be listened to and followed, creating a status of "micro-celebrity" in your niche.

Here is a quote from an undefined marketing guru source that stuck in my mind ever since I heard it "***MONEY FLOWS TO STATUS AND CELEBRITY.***"

When you are using the online space for marketing, mastering your voice opens up invitations to feature on podcasts, livestreams, and summits, exponentially expanding your reach to new audiences. This is a KEY to attracting clients consistently!

Unfortunately, in reality, grabbing attention and evoking interest in what you are saying is not always as easy. Often you may feel unheard, unseen, and your ideas not acknowledged or misinterpreted. WHY does this happen?

More persistently, this may happen because deep down, you are AFRAID to be unheard. And surprisingly, the more you try to attract attention, the less you usually get it.

In reverse, the less you care about the outcome of a specific talk, an interview, or training you give – the more positive comeback it brings!

I was recently invited to speak at a small online private event. It was a Saturday Breakfast Club kind of thing aimed at empowering members with inspirational stories. I was not asked to speak on Marketing or Human Design topics but to share how, throughout my whole life, I seem to make my craziest dreams my reality. Naturally, as I told my story, I mentioned discovering Human Design and how aligning my business and marketing with my energetics made a lot of very aligned shifts possible.

I certainly had zero expectations to attract clients – and yet within two weeks of the talk, my ROI on the time I spent with those ladies reached around €5000 as the majority of them joined my programs immediately. There were ONLY SIX PEOPLE on that call (and no replays.)

This is such a great example of how detaching yourself from the outcomes of your actions can fuel your visibility activities beyond what you can imagine.

The first rule of Visibility That Sells (and expressing yourself in a way that attracts clients) is to DETACH YOURSELF FROM EXPECTING INSTANT VALIDATION AND RESULTS.

The centre responsible for our self-expression and social integration of all the energy in our Design is the Throat Centre. All energy wants to move towards the Throat so it can be expressed and manifest itself through our voice.

**REMEMBER: The secret is NOT in the details when it comes to Living By Design. It is all in following your Strategy & Authority.** That is what aligns everything else, and truly this is a section I should have called "by popular demand" – it is something that feels super juicy, but it will not make any difference if you aren't interacting with people correctly and making authentic decisions.

I am creating this part only because people ask for more information, but I urge you not to get hooked up on it. This is not a "secret key" to attracting clients, just some ideas to lean into for your content. I want to inspire you with some ideas on how you can leverage this centre for your manifestation, creating what we call a Magnetic Brand Voice in conjunction with your Human Design profile lines expression.

So back to the Throat Center. Before you jump to any conclusions, having a defined Throat centre, even if you think it gives an advantage, is not a blessing. Let's look at both scenarios and what you can do based on whether you have that centre defined or not.

## If you have a DEFINED Throat Center

People with defined Throat centres are broadcasting specific set themes through their Voices. Like with any defined Centre, the themes exist in duality, which means they are really "black or white" by nature. When aligned and defined, the Throat has the gift of magnetism when speaking. When heavily conditioned, it actively feeds into the limiting belief that nobody can hear or understand you.

However, if your Throat centre is defined, you will generally be less likely to suffer from the fear of speaking. Does this mean that you do not need to work on your skills and master storytelling? Absolutely not!

In fact, the more you work on your speaking skills, the more opportunities that definition attracts in all areas of your life. Here are some ideas on what you could focus on:

• Take trainings and courses around the art of public speaking and storytelling.

• Try to plan your speeches. You do not need to script them - just make bullet points and let it flow.

• Work consistently on developing your unique speaking style and stick to it.

• Do live video challenges or create set topics/schedules for your video content marketing.

You have consistent access to your voice (a specific, consistent quality to your voice), and this ensures a level of confidence when you are speaking.

Your Throat Centre connects to more other centres compared to any other centre. Depending on which defined centres it is connected to by channels, you express a particular frequency of that centre and the channel that connects two defined centres.

• **Ajna** – you are here to **speak your mind (insights, opinions, ideas)**

• **Identity Centre (G-Centre)** – you are here to **speak authentically from your heart.** (Share experiences, make creative contributions, step into leadership and influence as the voice of others, and speak your truth)

• **Will (Heart or Ego Centre)**- you are here to **take leadership** (take charge and work independently)

• **Emotional Centre (Solar Plexus**) -you are here to **express feelings** (manifest through desires, articulate emotions)

• **Sacral** – you are here to manifest your **actions through your words** (you are here to **inspire and empower others to live their own truth**)

• **Spleen** -you're **speaking your intuition** (your survival wisdom, inspire others to **show up and be seen without fear**). (Through my 16/48 Channel, I hope to do this throughout this book.)

## What if you have an UNDEFINED Throat Center

If none of the channels leads to the Throat, it is generally recommended you wait for the right timing before speaking up with your opinion or advice. Does this mean you should give up on the dream of speaking confidently in front of an audience? Or create magnetic content? Absolutely NOT!

One of my favourite voices that I always feel most impacted by is the voice of actor Matthew McConaughey. When I looked up his Human Design, I was astonished that he has an undefined Throat Centre! When this man speaks, people shut up, listen (and enjoy themselves). Try his "Greenlights" in the audiobook version for a few hours of indulging in the pleasure of his sound and the accent and being inspired by the beautiful way he has to look at the world!)

An important observation, McConaughey does not ramble. He chooses what to say and how to say it, and – most importantly – WHEN to say it so brilliantly. Just take his infamous "Alright, alright, alright" line from Dazed and Confused. That one line made his whole career as an actor (which was not his intention at the time, and this role was an entirely accidental casting for a character who was not even supposed to speak). It became a viral catchphrase making its mark on the modern pop culture.

That power leaves me (a defined Throat Centre person) SPEECHLESS.

The openness of any Centre brings challenges. This is why people with undefined Throat Centre are more vulnerable to feeling unheard and having difficulty expressing themselves. And with self-expression, the Throat centre, when undefined, fuels the energy of self-doubt, leaving you feeling less confident and unable to make up your Mind about how to talk and what to say sometimes.

If your Throat Centre is undefined, you can still become an impactful, masterful, and captivating speaker, but you will need extra effort. So, what can you do to be heard when you speak and are recognised for your ideas and expertise?

Here are some suggestions:

• Face your fears- do not deny or ignore them.

• Speak when you are invited into the conversation, and you KNOW your opinion will be appreciated and considered.

• Try only talking about subjects/topics/ideas you feel solid in your knowledge of or passionate about.

• Master the art of expressing your point in fewer words. Do not allow yourself to ramble.

• Do not plan your speeches too rigidly. Allow space for improvisation & spontaneity.

You have a gift for adapting your voice to whoever you are talking to, energetically connecting to others with your voice. You draw people in like a magnet, making them feel seen, heard and wanting to hear what you have to say as a way of hearing what they have to say through you. You also have a gift of powerfully impacting others when the timing is right.

There is another crucial key for anyone with an undefined Throat Centre: learn to **TRUST YOUR SPEAKING ENGINE.**

Eric Edmeades is a serial entrepreneur and public speaker who was introduced into my world by a number of clients I guided. These clients were all certified in a nutrition program that Edmeades created called WildFit. After a couple of years, one of my clients invited me to take a 90-day WildFit Challenge, and it was finally an invitation that felt correct. The program was transformational, and I was pleased with my results, but I want to share something else even more powerful in this book.

During the program, a lot of material that keeps us on track are videos that Eric has recorded. For the first couple of weeks, we had to watch videos daily. Some of them were quite long – it really required dedicating a part of the day to consume that content. But time commitment did not become a problem – the content was deeply impactful, specifically because of what Edmeades has when he speaks: CHARISMA (in all caps).

I personally witness people getting entirely obsessed with him. I have to confess a slight obsession myself during the WildFit program. He is absolutely mesmerising when he speaks. he just pulls you in, and it is hard to fight it. (In contrast, my husband couldn't stand listening to those videos. Here is an example of what I wrote about earlier in the book: we are not for everyone, but the right people will always pay attention!)

And WildFit is not the only program he created. I explored some of Eric's other trainings, for example, on public speaking, business and marketing. My main goal wasn't to learn "how to run a business" – our business levels and nature are too different to get any actionable specifics. Still, I was so intrigued to watch him in action as a speaker and presenter, to watch how his influence works and specifically understand why it feels so powerful.

My Incarnation Cross of RAX Consciousness 3 (number 3 represents the Quarter of Duality – Purpose Through Bonding) is all about understanding how we bond for me. **Marketing and influence are all about bonding.**

Of course, I was so curious about Eric's Human Design, and at one point, could not resist boldly asking to run his chart. Eric Edmeads is a Pure (Sacral) Generator 6/2. Of course! He embodies everything I wrote about line 6 perfectly, showing up as a Role Model through his own experiences and stories.

The thing that shocked me the most was that he indeed had an undefined Throat Centre. What a great inspiration for anyone with a similar design who thinks they do not have the gift of speaking or grabbing attention.

Once, I was even granted access to watch him record a brand-new program. In the Q&A part, Eric was asked about the secret to his incredible ability to speak so well. Eric replied, "*Well, I just trust my speaking engine.*"

And this is all I ever needed to hear throughout all programs I watched that Edmeades created. This was **IT**!

I am here to pass it on to you and everyone with an undefined Throat centre: learn to **TRUST YOUR SPEAKING ENGINE** - it will create magic in your life.

## Grounding Your Voice

This section is not about selling by design. The Throat Centre is the centre of attracting attention, and it is the hardest thing to sell. This is why Ra Uru Hu placed it at the very bottom of the profitability list. This section of the book is more about leveraging what themes - activations - you have in your Throat centre and how you can ground yourself in it. These would be more natural, fixed ways to express yourself and make a point.

The best advice I have come across was from Robin Winn (in her book *Understanding the Centres in Human Design: The Facilitator's Guide to Transforming Pain into Possibility*. You can buy this book on Amazon if you want to learn more about the mechanics of Human Design Centres, although there is no business or marketing advice in it per se. Below, I am expanding on what I read in Robin's book.

To see what themes are fixed in your design - look at your hanging gates (the coloured Gates coming from your undefined Throat Centre):

**Gate 62. Details** – you are naturally inclined to dive deep into any situation's specifics and intricacies. You excel in analysing and dissecting information, seeking clarity and understanding by comprehensively examining the finer points. Your practical voice is rooted in your ability to identify and communicate the essential details that others may overlook.

You bring a valuable perspective to conversations and decision-making processes by grounding your voice in detail. You have a knack for spotting the nuances that can make a significant difference in outcomes. Your voice of reason cuts through complexity, allowing you to provide practical insights and solutions based on a thorough understanding of the specifics at hand.

Embracing the energy of Gate 62 enables you to communicate with precision and pragmatism. Your attention to detail ensures that your voice is well-informed and carries a sense of reliability and credibility.

Others look to you for practical guidance and appreciate your ability to break down complex ideas into manageable, actionable steps.

But I want to warn you that not every situation calls for an overwhelming focus on details. While your practical voice is valuable, there may be times when a broader perspective or a big-picture outlook is needed. Striking a balance between attention to detail and maintaining a broader perspective will allow your voice to be well-rounded and adaptable to different situations.

**Gate 23. Assimilation of Splitting Apart** – When you embrace this gate's energy, you possess a deep sense of wisdom and insight. You have a natural inclination to gather knowledge from various sources, allowing you to perceive different viewpoints and understand complex concepts. Your ability to assimilate information from diverse perspectives gives you a unique advantage in discerning the underlying truths and patterns that others may overlook.

To fully unlock the power of Gate 23, it is crucial for you to ground yourself in your own knowing. Trust in your intuition and inner guidance as you navigate through the vast sea of information available to you. When you stand firmly in your own wisdom, you can confidently share your knowledge with others, knowing that it is rooted in a deep understanding and personal truth.

It's equally important to be mindful of the timing when you choose to share your knowledge. Recognise that not every moment or situation is conducive to the reception of your insights. By carefully selecting the right timing, you ensure that your wisdom has the greatest impact, and you can make a significant difference in the lives of those around you. When you wait for the opportune moment, your words carry more weight, and your wisdom is more readily embraced and assimilated by others.

**Gate 56. The Storyteller** - As "The Storyteller," you have a natural gift for weaving narratives that captivate and engage others. Your ability to convey experiences, ideas, and emotions through storytelling is remarkable. You understand the impact of words and how they can transport listeners to different worlds, evoke deep emotions, and inspire profound insights.

To leverage this energy, it's essential to recognise that your storytelling power lies not only in the stories you tell but also in the skilful timing of when to share them. Choosing the right moment to unleash your tales amplifies their impact and resonance. You have an intuitive sense of when to speak up and when to hold back, allowing the energy of the moment to support and enhance the essence of your narrative.

When you align yourself with the appropriate timing, your storytelling becomes a potent force. Your voice carries weight, capturing the attention and imagination of your audience. Whether it's a personal anecdote, a metaphorical journey, or a tale with a deeper meaning, your stories have the ability to inspire, entertain, educate, and transform the lives of those who hear them.

**Gate 35. The Progress or Change** – This gate is about speaking from experience and engaging only in worthwhile adventures. When you align with the energy of this gate, you possess the wisdom to share insights rooted in your personal experiences, while also discerning which endeavours are truly meaningful and worth pursuing.

Your voice carries the weight of your own life experiences. You have a natural inclination to draw from your personal journey, reflecting on the lessons learned and the growth you have undergone. By speaking from this place of experiential wisdom, your voice becomes authentic, relatable, and enriched with valuable insights.

Your discerning nature allows you to navigate the vast array of opportunities and adventures that life presents. You have an innate sense of what truly matters and which paths are worth pursuing. Instead of aimlessly engaging in every endeavour, you exercise discretion, investing your time, energy, and resources only in those pursuits that align with your values and contribute to your personal growth.

**Gate 12. Caution** – This Gate highlights the significance of using your voice when you are "in the mood." You possess a unique sensitivity to the emotional spectrum. Your voice has the power to convey the intensity of both despair and elation, allowing you to express the depths of human emotions in a profound and authentic manner. When you tap into this energy and share your experiences, your voice becomes a vessel for genuine connection and understanding. Your voice is most impactful when you are genuinely "in the mood" and inspired to express the full range of your experiences.

The caution of Gate 12 reminds you to honour your internal state and timing when it comes to sharing your voice. By waiting for those moments when you are truly "turned on" and aligned with the energy of your experiences, you bring a heightened sense of authenticity and passion to your communication.

When you embrace this approach, your voice becomes a powerful tool for connection and transformation. Your words touch the hearts of others, allowing them to resonate with the depth of your emotions and find solace, inspiration, or validation in your shared experiences.

**Gate 45. King or Queen** – You possess inherent leadership qualities and a natural inclination to guide and educate others. Your voice carries the weight of authority, wisdom, and knowledge- making you an influential figure within your community or the groups you interact with. Your words hold the power to inspire, motivate, and uplift those who listen.

Being the voice of the teacher to the Tribe, it is crucial for you to ground your communication in leadership principles. Your voice is most impactful when it reflects qualities of confidence, clarity, and authenticity. By embodying these leadership traits, you command attention and respect, ensuring that your message resonates with the collective consciousness of the Tribe.

But there is a condition: timing plays a vital role in the effectiveness of your voice. Choosing the right moment to speak is essential to be truly heard and make a lasting impact. By observing and understanding the dynamics of the situation, you can identify the opportune time to share your wisdom and insights. This strategic approach ensures that your voice is received with openness and receptivity, maximising its influence and reach.

**Gate 33. Privacy and Retreat** - You have a natural inclination towards introspection and taking time for a personal retreat. You find value in withdrawing from external stimuli to delve deep into your thoughts and experiences. Through this process of reflection, you gain valuable insights and lessons from the past, allowing you to evolve and grow.

Your voice carries the weight of these reflections and the hope for improvement in the future. Ground yourself in reflecting on the past with the hope of improvement in the future. Choose the right timing to share your insights, ensuring that your words are received with receptivity and have a meaningful impact. By doing so, you become a source of guidance and inspiration, guiding others toward personal growth and positive transformation.

**Gate 8. Contribution** - Grounding yourself in authenticity is key to embodying the energy of Gate 8. Your voice carries the power of genuine expression, allowing others to connect with your authenticity and feel inspired to embrace their own. By speaking from your heart, sharing your own creative contributions and being true to yourself, you create a ripple effect that encourages others to do the same.

But remember, true support requires active listening and understanding. By attentively engaging with others' ideas, perspectives, and aspirations, you can tailor your support to their unique needs. Your voice becomes a source of guidance, offering valuable insights and feedback while honouring the individuality and creative vision of each person. Your voice becomes a force for collective upliftment and empowerment.

By recognising and supporting the creative contributions of others, you contribute to a harmonious and thriving community. Your authenticity inspires authenticity in others, fostering an environment where everyone can fully express their unique gifts and make a meaningful impact.

**Gate 31. Democratic Leadership and Influence** – You possess a natural gift of democratic leadership. Your voice carries the power to advocate for the collective, representing the needs and perspectives of the people around you. By setting aside personal ego and biases, you become a conduit for inclusive and fair communication, fostering harmony and unity within your community.

Speaking as the voice of the people requires patience and timing. You must wait for the right moment, allowing the energy and circumstances to align in a way that maximises the impact of your words. By observing the flow of events and sensing the needs of the collective, you can discern when it is appropriate to share your insights, guidance, and influence.

The essence of Gate 31 lies in prioritising the greater good over personal agendas. Your voice becomes a catalyst for democratic decision-making, empowering others and promoting fairness. By patiently waiting for the right time, you ensure that your message is received with receptivity and genuine consideration. Through grounding in this energy, your voice becomes a powerful instrument of influence and positive change. By speaking as the voice of the people, free from ego-driven motives, and waiting for the right time to share your wisdom and guidance, you contribute to the greater good of your community and inspire others to do the same. With patience and discernment, you create a harmonious and balanced environment where everyone's voice is heard and valued.

**Gate 20. In The Now, the Collaborator** - Your voice is most powerful when it emerges from a place of presence and awareness. When spoken IN THE NOW. With the gift of knowing when to manifest power, you are here to inspire others and connect people and resources. You have a natural ability to be fully present in the here and now. Your voice carries a unique vibrancy that captivates and engages those around you. By speaking from the present moment, you bring a sense of authenticity and immediacy to your communication, making a lasting impact on others.

You have the gift of knowing when to manifest power. You are here to inspire others and connect people and resources. Your voice becomes a conduit for building bridges, fostering collaboration, and facilitating the flow of ideas and opportunities. By recognising and nurturing the talents and strengths of those around you, you contribute to collective growth and success.

**Gate 16. Enthusiasm** – You naturally exude enthusiasm and charisma. Your voice carries an infectious energy that draws people in, making you a captivating communicator. However, to truly establish credibility and gain the respect of others, it is vital for you to ground your enthusiasm in mastery.

Mastery is achieved through dedicated practice and repetition over time. It involves immersing yourself in the subject matter, honing your skills, and developing a profound understanding of the intricacies involved. When you invest the necessary time and effort to become an authority in your field, your enthusiasm becomes authentic and well-founded.

While your ability to "wing it" may initially capture attention, it is your depth of knowledge and expertise that will hold the audience's interest in the long run. When you speak from a place of genuine mastery, people recognise your credibility and are more likely to listen intently to what you have to say. Your enthusiasm becomes a powerful tool to inspire and motivate others as they perceive your passion and expertise shining through. Only then, when you speak - they listen!

The above grounding practice suggestions require consistent practice and implementation, so be kind to yourself and do not expect an immediate result. The key is to learn your TIMING and read the room to ensure the people in your audience are open to your ideas. Less is more, and the quality of what comes out of your mouth over its quantity is crucial.

But here is the main thing. In reality, **you naturally require so much less attention** than those with a defined Throat Centre. And often, you are "trying to be heard" too hard because you are simply tricked into thinking that you need to grab that attention by your Mind.

It is forcing you into saying much more than you intend. When you fully let go of trying to "grab attention" and honour the timing and the quality of what you want to say, you will naturally become incredibly engaging, impactful, and magnetic to your audience.

# Chapter Twenty-Five

# A Personal Brand With An Undefined Identity Center? Yeah, Baby!

## Do Not Make Assumptions Based On One's Definition!

Recently, I was told by one client that according to what she learned from another trendy Human Design for Business coach, if the G-center( also known as Identity Center) in your chart is open or undefined, you should not be building a personal brand-based business.

To me, this statement is shocking, to say the least - simply because the evidence speaks otherwise.

In simple terms, the G-Center is a centre of direction and loveability. A person with a defined G-center tends to be much more stable or fixed in their path in life. They tend to have a strong sense of self, of being "somebody" - their identity.

But does this mean that a person with an undefined or completely open G-center does not know who they are? Not at all. My own life experience proves the opposite.

A sidenote and a warning. We need to be much more discerning about who we follow and listen to and be aware that personal chemistry can easily overpower the quality of their "expertise."

Human Design is going mainstream, which means there will be many more people trying to monetize this knowledge in the coaching industry. Their understanding of the basics is often very surface-level, and their strategies (or claims of success) are at times, quite questionable.

Take it from the Queen of Visibility. How we look online and what happens in our accounting books are not always the same reality. It is incredible when they are aligned, but very often, the visibility presells an impression that is not backed up by facts, and since "money flows to status and celebrity," impressive-looking visibility can help re-align the financial side of the business over time, but high earnings is not a given.

Even when we assume that the claims are correct, only because one person made it in their business does not give them any expertise on how to build a business as something to teach, especially under the light of Human Design, which is becoming a trend. The Human Design principle is simple: what works for one person could be grossly incorrect for the other. Hence, it is everyone's own experiment in life and in business to figure out what will work for THEM - by trying and testing various approaches for prolonged periods to see if they are truly aligned and profitable. No one can tell them what to do and how, EVEN Human Design experts. We can only suggest some ideas to play with.

Unfortunately, too many people believe very disempowering statements without questioning them or doing even some top-level research. Please, be very discerning about who you trust (and invest with).

## Personal chemistry is a powerful seller!

Let's look at the topic again. I have an undefined G-center. While I have been running my own business since 2012, my online visibility only started attracting clients when I decided to market myself as a personal brand. Before that, I would get all my clients locally through referrals, but online the story was very different. My Facebook page and website resembled an abandoned town in an old Western film, with tumbleweeds rolling around in the dust.

When I started showing up as ME, not my company, and I openly shared about myself and what inspired me - very quickly, a very distinct brand image formed, and it has been attracting clients without fail ever since. At the start, it was heavily influenced by who I watched and aspired to be like. And it kept evolving (and it is still evolving), but it definitely brought new clients into my world, those who wanted me to guide them after reading my content around visibility and building a powerful presence online. I was walking my talk and inspiring others. Creating. Connecting. Inspiring and empowering others to do the same. That is what personal branding is all about.

So why would anyone say that openness in the Identity Centre can be a problem for building a personal brand? If there is anything I found incredibly accurate is that openness does not mean a lack in any shape or form. In fact, when I wrote about the Throat Center, I mentioned people with such influential and unique voices. For example, Matthew McConaughey, who has an undefined Throat Centre, and specifically Vince Vaughn, whose Throat Center is entirely open. Have you ever met a wittier, faster-to-respond (or speak) person? I get that there is a script, but in many movies, the impro makes the final cut a lot. The best parts, in my opinion, and superb comedy at times. The Wedding Crashers is definitely one of our family favourites. The monologue at the beginning, when he talks about dating, cracks me up every time. I simply cannot do THAT with my defined Throat.

So getting back to the undefined or an open G-Center - it has nothing to do with not knowing who you are, not being able to create a magnificent and very distinct personal brand, or not being good at messaging (on the basis that "they do not have a sense of identity"). Unlike some programs or coaches may suggest. It is about being flexible in the way you show up and express yourself. It is about the influence of your environment and how you amplify and adapt and often outgrow it, too.

In my opinion, this is some sort of distortion of the original teaching around openness in the G-Center. Personally, I never wonder about "who I am." I always had a strong sense of direction, maybe because I am Splenic, so I am naturally intuitive, and I trust my journey - but the trajectory of that direction for me looks very different to someone with a defined G-Center. It is more of a chaotic zigzag line than a straight one - I cannot "settle" in one environment or identity for too long. I constantly evolve and change, and grow. People who knew me thirty years ago will not be dealing with the same person now.

Fifteen years ago, I even looked like a different person. I had an entirely different colour profile and personal style archetype (hair, clothes, style - an understated biker chick) than it is now.

I am also open to the idea that in 20 years, I can transform again. However, it feels like the direction within is only getting stronger as I move through these identities. But I am still the same person inside and very solid in being ME at that.

My brand undergoes constant upgrades. Like a caterpillar, I step into the new version of myself, and then, by the time the "back legs" catch up, my front ones are in the next - upgraded- version again. And it only adds to the way I can express myself, the flexibility and various roles I can play, and how I can show up and still fit into what Juliette Stapleton is.

A person with a defined G-Center perhaps does not need so many changes. They can have a more consistent presence/vibe/general branding. And those with undefined and open G-Center may be conditioned to feel they need to find that solid "final" brand or voice too. Yet our beauty is ever-evolving, not solidity.

And I love that, too. I love that we can lean into being so free to choose, literally daily, who we want to be at that moment. Before every Zoom client call and every podcast guest appearance, I would think of what I want to present myself as today, and I just adore putting on a specific "persona". In no way does it change who I am deep down or how I communicate.

And frankly speaking, we have to admit that nothing works in isolation. We just cannot talk about one centre without the influence of other centres in our design, specifically the defined ones. I already referenced my defined Spleen here. So there are no explicit black-and-white angles here. Yet it kind of triggered me to hear that someone who enjoys massive success in my industry due to being an excellent content creator actually cuts down some beautiful "flowers" by telling them they should not focus on their "show." Listen to me. If you have openness in your G-Center, a personal brand is where you will be most empowered.

Why? Because this means there ARE NO RULES! You are who you are, and "they" will have to take it or leave it. And we all know that if "they" want to leave it... "they" were not correct for us in the first place, so... who cares, right?

To empower you even further, here are some people with incredible personal brands that have an undefined or open G-Center:

- David Bowie
- Prince
- Princess Diana
- Kim Kardashian
- Elon Musk
- Steve Jobs
- Barack Obama
- Denzel Washington
- Robbie Williams

I should have you convinced at mentioning David Bowie and Prince. What an extraordinary example of people with such potent personal brands. Even if their style and looks changed over the years, they were still - very distinctly - David Bowie and Prince.

Yes, many people with undefined G-Center still feel like they need to "define" themselves before they are ready to show up, but this is just intense conditioning at play. The openness in this centre in no way stops us from showing up powerfully and leading with our personal brands, becoming extraordinarily successful and distinct in who we are.

Human Design is supposed to be an experiment - primarily focusing on following your Strategy and Authority, which activates all the goodness within and helps us decondition from all those shoulds and should-nots. You must play with it and take all the knowledge beyond that with curiosity, but not as a dogma to follow. If you do, you are only conditioning yourself into something else.

And so, I don't know about you, but as a person with an undefined G-center, I feel that my personal brand is as powerful as it can possibly be.

# Chapter Twenty-Six

# Selling From the Openness

*"The first thing I want you to understand is something very simple: You make money out of the not-self. You make money through the not-self; that is, the not-self brings material benefit to you. This is one of the great jokes of money courses.*
*...to teach any of this is really ugly in a way. The fact is the way in which we make money, the way in which we profit, is that we profit at the expense of the Not Self. And we profit by reinforcing the Not Self. I'm a realist. I accept that. I accept that the world is Not Self and will stay Not Self for a very long time. It is what it is; what to do. Acceptance is part of the way."*

Ra Uru Hu "The 64 Material Ways" p.3, 174

As much as this title may appear very juicy (you might have skipped the whole book to get here), I want to start with one simple fact: making money and selling something is never an act of "alignment." It is just the reality of the material plane we live in. To sell in your business, focus on your open centres and pay attention to the flavour they add to your messaging.

If you think about the bottom line of marketing, the successful triggers are always based around the "pain point," - which means we only take action when we want to change badly. I like the analogy with vitamins vs painkillers. I myself always forget to take vitamins consistently, as what they help with never feels like a pressing issue. Yet when my migraine comes, I RUN to grab something to calm it down. And it is just in our nature to take action when the change we need is causing discomfort. OR the desire we have started burning so intensely that we are experiencing the discomfort of staying where we are. We CRAVE the change. And ironically, from a Human Design stance, it is only Not Self that craves change.

When you are aligned, you feel so much more at peace, and you are happy. You do not need to change anything. But the world is not ideal. Gradually floating between Not Self and True Self is such a normal thing. Not every decision we make will be made strictly from our Inner authority, and we probably will always feel like we want more, better, and happier than what we are. Therefore, marketing will always succeed if it addresses the Not Self themes (cravings/pain points).

Here is an important point: the **definition** in your Design is what you consistently experience and bring into the world, and this is what your clients experience in your presence and through your business. But it sometimes means that you are only experiencing a small segment of a full possible spectrum of the theme in each area. Another issue is that seeing the world through a fixed perspective means you only understand how to approach it through that lens. You will also find that it is so natural to you that often, it is hard to articulate.

Where you are **undefined** is where your superpowers are, as you are likely to be very familiar with these Not Self themes. You can articulate them as these are areas your Mind is very hooked up on in its conditioning. Provided you are building your awareness around them (de-conditioning), and provided that what you do in your business is done with integrity and facilitates authentic transformation - you can focus your "selling" topics on talking from your openness, addressing the Not Self themes and your own mental conditioners in your content. THIS is what makes your marketing very magnetic and energetically triggering to take action and go deeper into the possibility of working with you.

I go into the details of each open centre and the hanging gates determining specific themes inside every Marketing Blueprint By Design™ report - **order yours at marketingbyhumandesign.com**

# Chapter Twenty-Seven

# Recognition By Design

## It Always Starts From Within...

Recognition is such a crucial success factor in Human Design. This chapter brings a deep dive into this topic, with some personal examples and insights to help you gain a very healthy and empowered approach to the topic of Recognition, I trust.

I am a Projector, and Recognition is a big part of my Design strategy. Projectors need to wait to be invited into relationships and ventures that are correct for them, where they can live out their true potential. But these invitations can only happen when others recognise you, and not just for you for whatever they think you are brilliant at. They need to see and recognise a specific contribution, a specific gift they see, the gift that follows a bigger calling inside you. Only then will you feel successful (your alignment signature).

Everyone has a specific gift they are here to be recognised for – and this gives us an amazing way to determine who are correct people in our lives and who are not, especially clients. Does each individual client or prospect see you for what you want to be recognised? Or is it some other thing they see that does not matter to you that much, so you do not actually feel fully SEEN by them (here is exactly the reason to get bitter and resentful for a Projector.) If you are a Projector, it is very important to get clear on exactly what you feel SEEN for, and then when you meet people that don't give you that specific Recognition, it is easy to say NO to them. There will also be no trauma, resentment, or bitterness in that.

To illustrate, here is an example. My background is in digital marketing and web design. I still get people asking me to help them with their website or guide them on how to grow their audiences on Facebook. Yes, this is part of what I can do and have extensive experience with. But if they do not see what I am REALLY here to do, it feels like I am almost invisible to them as a guide - they just want some information or need me to get something done on their website. And everything that could potentially transform their businesses that I suggest falls on deaf ears.

I promised myself never to work with those who do not see me. It does not feel sweet to me and is not worth my energy. This is a wrong recognition that does not make me feel successful at all. Instead, it triggers bitterness and takes over everything in my life: my creativity, my well-being, and my motivation. I cannot afford and simply refuse for this to happen anymore.

If I can guide people, especially with marketing and messaging, and if I can empower them, I want people in my world ACTUALLY to recognise that I've empowered them. From that, they can NOW take action, and NOW they have a huge breakthrough. NOW they have become so clear within themselves in their content and in the way they attract clients.

It's not about even how many clients they will get when they are working with me. I know they will, and I do not need to add "get X number of clients every week" into my messaging to attract them. This is not what I specifically guide through, and I do not want clients to expect this specific outcome from working with me.

What matters to me is that they are "injected with success": empowered, expanding their reach, creating this shiny cover for their visibility, and then growing into it. As they do, they become "THAT BIGGER VERSION" of themselves and can start creating an even bigger one. It is the story of my life- creating a bigger version, putting it online, and then growing into it at my own pace. This is what I'm guiding others into as well. It's important for me that people recognise me for that kind of empowerment, not something else. It is so vital to know what you feel good to be recognised for. It will help you articulate clearer in your marketing messaging too.

So many energies in us require Recognition to be perceived correctly by others. To make a difference that we are inspired to make. Sometimes we express ourselves without consciously thinking about the mark we leave. If you are a 1/3 like me, for example, your impact happens through your introspective research and discoveries. It is not that you do it to influence others. You do it to have a breakthrough and gain a solid understanding of the foundation of things. But by sharing what you find, it is impacting others.

It is all about you being on purpose, embodying that specific energy you seek to be recognised for. That clear specific recognition that makes you feel your alignment for success if you are a Projector, or satisfaction for Generators and Manifesting Generators, or peace for Manifestors, or surprise for Reflectors. So, recognition is a very, very specific thing. And YOU need to be amongst people who see yourself for that "thing."

## The Right Timing

I want to talk about the right conditions for the recognition. What can you do? What can you be in charge of to be indeed seen and recognised BEFORE you can act, speak, help, or offer guidance?

The need to wait to be first recognised and invited to speak or guide is something that is not limited to Projectors. So many gates and channels in the bodygraph have this condition for their gifts to be expressed correctly. The whole notion of "projected energy" is fascinating to me and is paramount for your awareness of why you need to make yourself available for that recognition. As well as why "waiting" is essential as part of this process - especially if you are a coach or an expert guiding others through some form of transformation.

It is all about how you can never be recognised if you are expressing yourself in the wrong place in front of incorrect people or at the incorrect timing. There will be repercussions.

For example, if you have a line 5 in your profile (5/1s and 5/2s are the worst affected), it can damage your reputation if you're saying something at the wrong time. People can easily misunderstand what you're saying and straightaway project their anger or other negative emotions onto you. So, you need to be discerning and wait for the right timing to speak or do something.

A great example is Sinead O'Connor, a 5/1 Manifesting Generator, famously ripping the Pope's photograph at a nationally broadcasted US event. It was the wrong timing for her, people did not expect this, and they lashed back at her with such force it affected her reputation and the course of her whole life in a negative way. If she chose another stage or setting for the same act, somewhere the audience was more open- or had been informed to recognise her and the generational pain she represented with this gesture - she could have become one of the world's leaders. Watch the documentary called "*Nothing Compared*" to see her story and irreversible projections switch in action. It is so deeply moving, and it is poignant to show how vital the right timing is for a line 5 person.

Or let's look at 1/8 The Channel of Inspiration- connecting the G-Centre (channelling your Higher Self) to the Throat centre. It is so interesting how this channel works because its energy kicks in when you get an idea, a divine inspiration, and sometimes your idea will defy any logic. Since we're living in a world that is defined by logic, when you get this idea, you can only express it in front of people who recognise you for a particular talent, gift, or quality you have. Only then will your illogical idea be heard and perceived correctly.

## Setting Up Your Stage

One area to look at is when you're showing up as the face of your business and you choose your main visibility platform. Somewhere where you can "drive your traffic" to and where they can consume your content. Preferably "binge" on it without getting distracted. This is where you can set the stage to nurture those who recognise you to become your clients.

In my personal story, which is, of course, not a directive on "how to do things" in general because it is about my unique experience and my energetics, my platform was my Facebook personal profile for many years. I have built my audience and my visibility and have acquired a lot of expertise with Facebook organic marketing, mostly on what doesn't work. As a 1/3 profile person, I tend to take on tactics full-heartedly, and after a while, by experiencing them first-hand, I often start seeing through the smoke screen of conditioning. I realised that most of the tactics we are taught are unnatural regarding how we interact in social scenarios. As such, I kind of learned what works for me by a process of elimination.

But since I discovered Human Design, I could see how some of the tactics I was so focused on were entirely misaligned with my unique Design. It explained not only why I did not enjoy doing these things on a daily basis. It shone a light on what I was so afraid to admit to myself: why they brought so few results compared to the effort required. And then, I started looking at my clients' Designs and seeing why the same tactics were very successful for some of them. This was when I found my compass, the tool to guide myself and my clients toward what can feel much more natural for them. And I walked my talk by slowing down massively and stopping the hustle tactics altogether. At the end of the day, I had to experience experimenting with my Design in business first-hand to really know if it actually works.

It was a very scary decision to stick to, but my Inner Guidance, my Splenic Authority, gave me the KNOWING that I should trust this process. Slowing down created space and clarity, allowing me to re-evaluate my actions. I started focusing more on evergreen content, turning my website into a "hub" where those who find me through all of my external visibility efforts can come and immerse themselves in my insights and perspective. I then created just one very simple free training to offer a taster for those who need one and offered a one-off strategy service that would serve me as a "pre-qualifier" for clients to experience my guidance and invite me to guide them. It also allowed me an opportunity to experience them in a working environment and "feel" if I even wanted to continue. In other words, if their invitation was the correct one for me.

Here are a few immediate benefits these changes brought to my business...

Clarity on the exact path one needs to take on my website to become a client. The amount of mental space this clarity gives is priceless. Obviously, I did my research on what feels the juiciest as an entry-level paid offer, and I created something that leaves clients pleased with the value they get.

Replacing free discovery calls about my long-term mentorship programs with a paid offer that included a strategy call - filtering correct and incorrect people while getting paid. Such a win-win scenario for me - saving my energy but providing me with the sweetness and the feeling of security of having monetised my efforts and time. In fact, the menu on my website only displays the details of my other programs when they are launching for new members intakes, but never for the eyes of those who just came across me. They have to go through the funnel I created first.

I had already experienced several scenarios when individuals wanted to have a call with me about working together, and I insisted that they order the one-off service first. Half of those people ended up not being the right people for me. I could feel it almost immediately during the strategy sessions, and I was so glad I got paid for the time I spent with them. Everything I do in my business is aimed at eliminating any potential bitterness. As a Projector, bitterness has a paralysing effect on my creativity. I cannot afford it - and that is the bottom line.

Clarity on where and how I am driving all traffic to - from my social media platforms, my podcast, guest appearances on other people's video content, or features in the press. Clarity on what steps those warmed-up leads take to become my clients or part of my Inner Circle inside my longer-term mentorship.

Finally, a more relaxed way to trust my business and know exactly what I need to do more of and where I can use more automation and hustle less. Which is, ironically, the place I spent so much effort on in the years prior to running my business by Design. Now all I have to do is watch out for conditioning that makes me sometimes feel guilty that I work so little and get paid "all that." Funny, right? I did everything to find that freedom and flexibility in my business - only for my Mind to try and sabotage me and tell me I am too laid back. Thankfully, I know these thoughts are just thoughts, and they are not ME or my TRUTH.

When I niched down and added Human Design to my guidance, I started pouring my insights and discoveries into blogging because I noticed that one of my articles started ranking on Google. I saw clearly how it's important that, first of all, I focus on discoverability. This made my marketing much more effective and efficient. This is very strategic. This means that I'm only attracting people who are looking for a particular answer to a particular question. And I offer them pieces of content that answer those questions.

When they find me, they get exposed to more content AND my introductory offers too. All in one place - on my website. I often call my website my "castle." It is the platform for me best to shine and where I am available for correct Recognition. It is where I can bring the correct people closer into my world. They get to consume a lot of "me" and take the next step. Only then do they get invited into my exclusive Facebook group, where I like to stay connected to my past and present clients, but without any agenda.

It is not in my nature to hustle in a Facebook group, as we already know. But when I have something to say (or sell), I have a group of people who are very aligned with me to share what I have on offer.

My current marketing strategy is the opposite of what I did for years, which was driving all my connections to my Facebook profile, hoping they will read my brilliant posts, only to lose their attention to a funny kitten reel. Now, on my website, if there is something that "distracts" my reader, it is probably an invitation to order a **Marketing Blueprint By Design™ report from me (at https://marketingby**

**humandesign.com.)**

I know not every one of these people who enter my inner circle will be "my people" 100%. For example, as I mentioned, not everyone, after ordering a report, will be invited even to consider the opportunity to be in my Visibility That Sells Accelerator, my inner circle mentorship program, and have me as their guide. I used to be much more open and available for anyone to join my programs, but then I ended up attracting people who did not recognise me for what I needed because they were not taking action with my guidance, and I didn't see any impact for which I wanted to be recognised. And that is a big, big thing for me. I don't want to be "paid for chats" - unless they inspire action.

## Creating A Safe Space for Your Visibility

On social media, curating your audience is essential to feel safe and attract people who see and recognise you. But how do you do that?

First of all, learn about your energetics, what is correct for you and what is incorrect for you by Design. You are not for everyone, and not everyone is for you. If anybody in your audience is simply a very wrong person – you will know exactly who they are. You can, and you have the power to let go of them intentionally.

Would you like to know how I deal with that on Facebook? Very simply!

Disclaimer, everything I suggest best suits someone who is a coach or an expert and uses their Facebook profile for connecting to others and building their visibility. This advice is not applicable if your business representation only uses your Facebook business page. Still, you might find my thought process useful.

If someone is out of line on my own posts, I BLOCK them. I basically deny them the right to even see into my existence. I find that very empowering. I do not need to bend backwards for anyone who does not SEE me. I do not need to apologise for my decision to eliminate them from my world. I do not need to "work on myself" to be a "better person."

It is all just "black or white" for me; they are either correct or incorrect. That is the choice I advise you to base your decision on if in doubt. If someone lets themselves be known as really incorrect, perhaps leaving inappropriate comments or messages – I block them, just like that. No excuses. If I allow an incorrect person to still be in my world in some capacity, it's like I'm cutting off my wings. By being in my space, they take away my ability to fly. So, my block list is huge, and it feels good. (That is partially my line 3, "breaking bonds" and loving it, by the way.)

Some people might be incorrect in lesser ways, and sometimes blocking is a step too far. Maybe they haven't crossed the line, or I did not feel energetically repelled just yet. When I spot that, I can unfriend them if they are just random connections or allow them to still be my Facebook friends, but I unfollow them. Out of sight - out of mind.

What I see on my feed is in my control. When someone stirs unpleasant feelings with their content, I do not have to continue seeing their posts. I have some people who I know and like on a personal level, but their content is somewhat incorrect for me. I just unfollow them - creating space for those who inspire me (I mark them as my See First contacts) and creating space where I can feel good showing up.

I no longer see their content, although maybe they're still watching me. I know there are some people who I was in close interaction with before, and I still see them occasionally commenting on some of my posts. But I don't engage with their comments, don't ever message them or reply to their messages, if any (or if I have to, I reply with a one-liner without further engaging.)

You CAN "switch off" that person in your life. You have the right to – you don't owe anything to anyone. In my view, the only thing you're here to care for is the connection to yourself and to the ones that ARE correct for you.

Sometimes, there are triggering events in the world that get people a little too expressive, or you just got tired of someone and want to test if they are triggering you or if something else does. Either way, when someone temporarily creates not-so-correct energy, you can SNOOZE them for 30 days. Facebook has all those options.

However, **you don't owe anyone any of your time.** That's wasting it, and that is the greatest, in my opinion, attitude to have in terms of understanding that need to "wait to be recognised" to express some of the ideas, to speak. You are not timidly waiting to be noticed. You decide WHO gets the privilege of experiencing YOU.

## Knowing The Right Timing

We looked at the need to wait to express yourself if your design tells you that you have some of those energies. But it is not anything to do with creating content for your online visibility. It's about talking to another person or a group of people in person (or virtually, on a group call). It's about when the other people are directly involved.

It is the same with Manifestors, for example. A Manifestor will get resistance when they're directly affecting another person because that's an aura interaction. And they have a closed (repelling if they do not consider how others feel it) aura. When they enter the room, their aura is so dense already, so when they do something unexpected by others, it feels almost threatening, and so they are met with resistance. Everything happens on that subconscious energetic level. It is not even a conscious thing regarding how we feel each other's auras.

Manifestors need to wait for the inner clarity where they feel that creative spark can be acted upon but need to inform anyone involved before the action happens. Soften the energetic impact a bit and get them on board by letting them know what is about to happen.

But Manifestors do not need to inform others that they are about to express themselves on social media, for example. If they want to create content about whatever their creative sparkle is, whatever they want to express, they can just go and do it. No informing required. Sometimes they miss this massive point. It is only by having the courage to allow themselves to do that freely that they get a chance to be recognised.

Where they need "to inform" is in their call to action. This is where just saying *"Do this"* is not enough. Inform others about the process it involves, which can happen in the form of simply explaining step by step how a reader or a viewer can take the next step in their funnel. It may feel weird to have to spell it all out, but this is one way your strategy to inform works. When you see how this is helping to remove the resistance and bring more people into your calls or programs, it may even become your favourite thing to do!

I will never stop repeating that nobody needs to wait for recognition before creating content for their visibility, marketing, and business. This is how we attract people who see and recognise us correctly in the first place. This is what we do while waiting. Waiting is never a passive act of sitting on your hand and hoping for a miracle. We can create the foundation for the recognition to happen.

Recognition, the true kind, opens the hearts and the minds of people to us. We can share and know that what we share impacts others correctly.

And when we cannot ensure we have that recognition when directly interacting with people, we need to think twice if sharing is worth it.

For example, as a Projector, I need to be recognised in order for another person to receive my guidance. Whenever I see a discussion, let's say in a Facebook group, and there's a question or a statement that draws me to offer my perspective or guide them or show them a different view, I am aware that my energy (especially in those passionate moments where I feel the pressure to share) can be very heavy to receive. In the past, I was in situations where my reply was not received well at all, and I would feel bitter and resentful about not being perceived correctly. But they did not ask me for THAT much guidance. They did not SEE me as someone they recognised, and so my energy appeared way too heavy for them. They don't have the recognition of my brilliance as a guide.

Now, with some of my clients who really do recognise me for the right thing, I can go in as heavy and as direct as it gets (and I am a very straightforward and direct person.) I don't like mind games, and I'm very bad at them. So, I just like I say it as it is, and they can receive it. And it is something they needed to hear at that moment. I feel seen and recognised as they often thank me for the breakthrough that happened there and then. I noticed it's safe for me to be direct, heavy and laser-sharp and to tell them exactly what the problem is. In some other scenario, if I wasn't recognised, this information would have landed in a challenging way, and there would be a real break-up in relationships, which could be damaging.

It is interesting to me to observe this whole thing about the correct recognition at play in my life and in the lives of people around me. How we always know who is correct and who is incorrect, but we let our mind and logic override our instincts -as we don't follow our Human Design Authority. As a Splenic person, my first impressions are the green lights or the red flags immediately. If the red flags are ignored, we get into these relationships that are not just mediocre - they are incorrect, dangerous, and can be detrimental to our well-being and health. You deserve nothing less than amazingly correct for you, and that's what I want for you too.

I want you to focus on the recognition that you are designed to attract. In that way, you have more and more people who recognise you for who you are and who you are for them.

# Chapter Twenty-Eight

# Slow Down To Accelerate

## Waiting And What to Do While You Are Waiting

As I mentioned many times in this book, waiting is not a passive process, but it is a crucial part of most people's Human Design strategy. Generators/Manifesting Generators need to wait to respond. Projectors are waiting for the correct invitations. Reflectors are waiting through the lunar cycle (or more). Manifestors are the only ones who can initiate, provided they inform. However, Emotional Manifestors need to wait for emotional clarity before making decisions. So waiting is everywhere, and the most shocking discovery for most people is that it is a good thing!

It is funny to me as I live near one of the city's main roads and I do not own a car (deliberately, so I can move more in my life). So, I get to cross that road a lot - literally every time I leave the house. When my husband was alive, he was always rushing to cross it, even when the lights were red. Les did have a defined Root centre, after all. But I always wanted to wait. For me, waiting is an opportunity to contemplate, to pause, and to take a deep breath (figuratively speaking, I try not to breathe in those horrid fumes, of course). A chance to slow down before I accelerate.

Waiting is a good thing, but how do we approach it when it is not just 30 seconds at the crossing? Well, to me, the simplicity of the answer is the most mind-blowing:

**GET BUSY!** Wait, Juliette, WHAT? Haven't you been telling us not to hustle all the time?

Yes, I have, and I will again, but I am not talking about that sort of busyness. Focus on what technically makes time fly and often reduces the time you need to wait. And sometimes you may even feel, *"Oh, I was enjoying the waiting part so much, is this moving too soon?"*

I have to pause and laugh here because that is exactly the voice of our Mind. Nothing is good enough. It is either too long or too fast. Yet, everything happens at the right time - if we wait for what we are waiting for correctly.

**Generators** - focus on self-discovery. Notice if you have available energy to take on a task. If no, just give it a little rest. Jump into things you love, roles you love to play in life and say YES to your passions that you have been putting aside to make space for others. Get SELFISH (in a good way) - make it about your SELF and WHO you are. Remember how everything happens for you, so you can figure out who you are? You are designed for this focus, and this will evoke that feeling of deep, deep satisfaction - doing what you love and being what you want to be.

**Projectors-** get your minds seduced by diving into studying and mastering the system. If you are drawn to something, allow yourself to go deep to really learn it inside out. Projectors need systems. If they do not understand the systems deeply, they are just confused and unsure. Whatever the system is - go deep. Just by losing yourself in the studying process, you unlock so much magnetism.

I am not joking when I say that the most important invitations in my life came to me when I was NOT looking and just diving deep into mastering something.

My husband came into my life when, after 27 promiscuous years, mostly initiating relationships and getting burnt out every time, I said to myself - NO MORE, and decided to put all my energy into studying music technology. On the very first class of the course I enrolled in, the lecturer walked in and immediately started talking to me. I did not even realise that this was my other half, the one I consciously looked for all my life since the age of three years old!

I was not even meant to master music technology but diving into it and giving up my obsession with finding my other half (in other words giving up NOT waiting) - delivered him almost immediately. And it was he to invited me into relationships when the course finished.

Actually, what I learned still serves me when I edit my podcast and video content. So, it all adds up.

**Reflectors** - the month of waiting is so good for you. There is no pressure. You can go about your life experiences and your daily personality/energy changes at your pace. No pressure. Everything works out and becomes clear to you when you allow that time to pass. Jump into what draws you. You may find yourself getting obsessed with this or that. Building strong beliefs only to wake up one day and drop everything you believed to be true to date. It is ok. This is a beautiful experience of LIFE. This is where your special wisdom is born from.

**Manifestors-** Gosh, what are you waiting for? Express yourself through whatever you feel you want to - just inform those directly involved. Use your powerful voice to share your ideas and your vision. And anyway, who am I to tell you what to do - focus within and just wait for your own creative sparks.

Waiting is so good when you are conscious about HOW to wait. And, of course, focus on sharing your experiences, insights, wisdom, and visions. I have given you so many pointers on how to find your own unique angle. Get insanely visible, but only in the way that makes you feel good showing up. Focus on creating your "castle" of visibility - and remember- a few bricks do not create a wall. And a couple of walls do not make a dwelling liveable. You are in for a long game, but what can be created while you are in the waiting process? (Which is never an A to B process.) It is like a helix, like your DNA, a spiral ascension that goes on and on and on. Not only is it beautiful, but it is also satisfying, successful, peaceful, surprising, and a hundred other things!

The most important note is that focusing on your visibility this way is so empowering. It helps you shape yourself into a much more expansive version of yourself, and it happens fast. If only back in 2017, when I started my online coaching journey, I knew how securely I would be showing up in just a few years - solidly confident in my skin, with my heart open to the world (just enough, of course, I am a "loner" and a very private person and all that); believing that my voice deserves to be heard the way I am; talking about Human Design; and contributing to the world's largest publications about it - I would never believe it. It would seem unattainable. Yet here I am.

Get busy showing up while you are waiting - the right way!

## Messaging Tip: Talk About What You Want Them To SEE

If you find that people recognise you for something that you don't want to be recognised for, create content around it. Talk about it, using statements like-

*"This is not what lights my heart."*

*"This is not what matters to me."*

*"Yes, there are so many things I can do well, but this is not where I feel like the most important recognition for me is. I am here to..."* and you express what you want to be recognised for.

Your content and messaging are powerful channels for communicating who you are, what you want to do, and who you want to attract. But it doesn't work when you follow some overused templates in your messaging or oversimplify when you are addressing your target audience by saying something like, *"If you're an entrepreneur, this is for you."*

I'm talking about expressing who you are and then letting the correct people actually see you for it. To see beyond those words and into your energy so that they can get to a point where they say, *"You are the guide for me to take me from this point A to point B."* By stating that you talk to entrepreneurs, you do not achieve anything. But by creating content that I resonate with on a deeper level and that I connect energetically with - you have got my attention!

## Getting Discovered & Monetising It

I have already given you an example of creating a simpler, reliable path to convert readers into clients on my website. But to bring them into my website, I focus on creating a variety of discoverable pieces of content - each of them serves me as a micro-funnel.

For example, if I want to talk about something really specific, like Human Design Environments – I will first see what people are Googling around this area. I research what has been created and how much brilliant competition there is already. Maybe there are so many excellent pieces that it's very difficult to compete with. Maybe I just need to narrow down the title or play with my topic a little bit in order to be discoverable. Often it is all about a little tweak in the wording of a title.

Even if you are not niching generally, you can create individual pieces of content niched down to answer a specific question or address a focused issue - one at a time.

I'm a Projector- focusing on mastering a system is paramount for my design. When I niched into marketing by Human Design, it transformed my business (proving that for my energy type and profile going deep is key). But there is another secret to what I create... I know that I can only create powerful content when I am "in the zone". If I am not there when I'm talking about something, there is no energetic appeal in my words. As such, all I'm doing is adding to the noise out there rather than expressing myself and my insights.

The ZONE is the condition that is a must when I create content these days. And I cannot plan for it. But what I create in the zone definitely attracts paying clients through my blog- so I have the evidence that less is more. Quality (energetically speaking, authenticity by design) is what makes my content compelling to the correct people.

So, this is how people find me – through niche discoverable topics that lead to my content through web search. From this, I have the added bonus of word of mouth and personal recommendations to others. NEVER underestimate the value and the power of word of mouth marketing.

I have another secret that works for me, and I already mentioned it. I do not make my freebie the first step in entering my marketing system.

It is not about building my email list because I noticed that only a tiny percentage of those who get my freebie convert into even the entry-level offer. And then I think about WHY they are signing up for that freebie. If I was in their shoes, which as a massive researcher I often am - what do I want when I sign up for a freebie? And my answer is - information. Do I want more support at that stage? Do I want a mentor or a coach? Absolutely not. I am just looking for information, and that is it. This is why the freebie does not convert. And you know what? I am so generously sharing the information inside that free training. It is OK. I know the right ones will stick around. But I do not need to send all my traffic to that training, knowing how low conversions are into a paid product.

Please keep in mind that we are all different and unique. This is how and what I discovered works for me and my unique design, lifestyle, values, and priorities in life. You are a unique person in your own way. I am merely demonstrating my way of doing things in this book as an example of focusing on ME versus what I SHOULD be doing because some guru says so.

In my blog, I deliberately use the call to action in my articles to lead my readers to what some marketers call a "foot in the door offer" (Not my favourite term, frankly speaking.) The ones that are ready to take that next step order a Marketing Blueprint By Design™ report. It is not a low-cost product either. It is a medium-cost product, and it's something that I try to overdeliver. I often give over 40 pages of dense text of really detailed, comprehensive information, plus a strategy session full of inspiration and guidance that they can take to experiment with the Design energetics in their businesses. Finally, they get my Visibility Expert Insights about how these energetics could show or be used when they're showing up for their online visibility, for their marketing, for working with clients, or for structuring their business.

Now, they are my clients. They have experienced my guidance already, and NOW I can curate their journey with me. I can either invite them to talk about investing in more support or, if the timing is not right, I can invite them into my Facebook group for clients to keep connected.

An interesting observation about having a Facebook group is that I'm not drawn to be active in the group because it's not in my nature. I think it is good to have a common place for all your clients. My group members don't care if I haven't posted anything for a month. They're not going to leave the group because of infrequent posting. All that "keeping your group engaged" is conditioning I no longer buy into. That was a "big one" to let go of.

I allow myself to go with my natural energies of just BE me. Yes, I like to have a group that sees me as a Guide, but I don't have to bend backwards as a group admin. I will come and guide them when the time is correct to speak when I feel like I have something to say. This is also my curated safe space to actually be open to someone who will listen to what I'm saying and go with me.

Although showing up in a more exposed environment like my personal profile was my choice before, I feel it is more appropriate to go deeper into my expertise in a designated space for it. This is why I focus on my website much more these days.

Showing up on social media is like a musician busking in the street, and those who love it stay and listen. However, the website is like a performance in the venue, where people go intentionally to listen to me - happy to buy a t-shirt after. We still need social media presence to let them know "the gig" is happening and to stay on top of people's minds, but I feel that it is so much harder work when you put all your "eggs" into that social media "basket." And it can be very discouraging to keep it up.

## Showing Up

Recognition is a really specific thing. And yes, every one of us can really curate who we will allow to SEE us. And I do not mean hiding from people; that is the opposite of what I'm trying to say. A lot of people are so afraid, and they're still looking for some sort of validation on the outside. They're still looking for answers to questions like, *"Is my voice good enough?"* or *"Should I take that person's structure and just try and tweak it to create something of my own based on that?"*

And there is nothing wrong with learning how brilliant people do things and then tailoring it to how you do things. That's how we learn – from observation. Therefore, it's not like blind copying, although that happens too. And that's not good because that's when you don't trust yourself. You can always get inspired by those other people or their content, but you still need to trust yourself and your voice to express yourself. You need to trust your energetic right to choose who to talk to.

For that, you need to be showing up. You can't be hiding.

Recognition will never happen if you're hiding. Recognition will only happen when you're showing up powerfully; when you trust in your voice; when you're not concerned about if this is the "right" structure or if it's the "wrong" structure; and when you just try things on, but you're not concerned that somebody says this is wrong.

Unless you're doing something incorrectly for YOU, and someone like me (your Guide) sees that and says, *"Hey, it feels like you were doing this wrong. You're trying to be someone else. But I want you to be yourself because you are brilliant."*

You ARE brilliant. And I admire you.

When you trust your Design, when you recognise yourself, it becomes effortless to be showing up with your Truth. This is when the right people can see and recognise that Truth in you -whatever role you are designed to play in their lives. They will call you out and crave you to guide them.

That's the kind of recognition I wish for you.

# Chapter Twenty-Nine

# What To Talk About?

## Creating Content for Your Marketing

Remember that the audience piece is critical – no matter what your Human Design is.

When you address a highly targeted audience, more people listen and show interest in your offers. When you speak to "the universe,"- which means you are just talking at a bunch of people who are not targeted and often ill-fit to your message- you are likely to get crickets in return. It is crucial to speak to your targeted audience in terms of engagement and attracting clients, even if you are the best speaker in the world!

So, make sure you work on the quality of your audience and your public speaking skills; both are equally important. Specifically, be intentional with who you connect on social media or who you are collaborating as a speaker with.

In your chart, have a look at your Throat Centre – are there any channels leading to it? Lean into the energy of the channel. And if you don't have the channels (which makes waiting for the right timing to speak very important for you), you can look at the active gates around your throat centre. Based on these, you can also use particular statements to really express this energy and magnetise your marketing messaging.

I go so much deeper into the energy of the hanging gates, especially in our open centres, inside **Marketing Blueprint By Design™ report, which you can order today at marketingbyhumandesign.com.**

When you are creating the actual content, quality is paramount, but here is where you should always follow your Human Design Type's Strategy & Authority:

**Projectors** create content when in the zone, around things you are really into. Never create anything just because you feel you are not "doing enough."

**Generators and Manifesting Generators** – create content when you respond to something on the outside, and it truly lights you up. Pro secret: it does not have to be about your business all the time. People work with people, and when you are lit up by something, that passion attracts the right people into your business through your personal magnetism.

**Manifestors** – create when you feel that creative spark. Do not think about what you should or should not be doing or whether you have the means to follow through with the idea all the way. Talk about ideas and inspirations that come to you so that you can ignite the rest of us into action.

**Reflectors** – work with daily transits to follow the strategy to the type that the transit allows you to tap in, depending on the planetary alignments, and then follow the advice above according to that type.

# Chapter Thirty

# Visibility 101 - Quick Tips

## My Fundamental Secrets to Creating Magnetic Content

I know I go a long way in expressing my points. It is a very common trait of people with 1/3 profiles, I have noticed. To summarise some of the juiciest points around content creation, I put together these quick tips. All of them were more or less covered at some point in the book.

**Secret #1: Only create when energetically lit up** - release the need to post daily unless you have already created a bank of "fillers." By "fillers," I am talking about things we build but sometimes forget to consistently show off. For example, testimonials; quotes created from what you often say to clients; past guest appearances on podcasts and online discussion shows; any of your past blog articles, or those you were featured in. Anything of value that can position you as an authority in your niche needs to work for you over and over again. Load them into your favourite automation software and give yourself some breathing space for creating content that matters.

And then it is a matter of having the discipline to create content when we feel that there is something that could be so good to share - feeling that fire inside and not doing it because you think you should. When we create content without being energetically lit up, we only add more noise into the already noisy space. When we create content from a place of passion, we create a connection with the reader - from the start!

And then, they stop the scroll and pay attention.

**Secret #2: Create evergreen content BEFORE social media content.** Focus on blogging, guest blogging, booking podcast appearances, or start your own podcast or an online video series. Interviews work very well, and they allow repurposing the content created in so many formats! That is how I created my visibility on Facebook back in 2017.

It all adds to your discoverability! As I just mentioned - once something is created, it can do the heavy lifting for your client's attraction again and again. In fact, when my husband got sick and passed away, I had to step back from creating anything in my marketing for three months. That is a quarter of a year! I did not create any posts for my business and allowed my automation software to repost my "filler" content and social media posts that were successful in the past. I always save them once I see they are good. This is not based on engagement but instead on how I felt when expressing my points through them. And I was shocked to hear from my accountant that those three months that I had to rely on my evergreen content were actually the strongest start of the year in my business ever.

It is crucial to have a long-term vision with your content creation strategy. All your efforts will pay off eventually, just do not attach expectations of immediate results to avoid burnout.

**Secret #3: Create discoverable (searchable) niche topics** for your blog articles/podcast episodes (even if you have a wider niche). You see, the more discoverable individual pieces of content you produce, the more likely the right people will find you. When we Google a solution for our problem, we do not use generic terms or some form of coaching language. It is crucial to figure out the words our clients use to ask questions about the issue or a topic that we are experts on.

And even if those words are slightly wrong, it is only by prioritising getting discovered over how fancy you want the name of your latest blog post to be that you have a chance to connect to and attract so many more people - and not just any people! Those who are actively seeking something you offer. In other words - warm leads!

**Secret #4: Lean into the energy of your Human Design Profile fully to express yourself.**

Release any self-shaming for talking about yourself a lot (especially if you are a 1/3 or a 6/2).

Embrace and take responsibility for articulating your promises clearly if you are a 5/1 and 5/2.

Focus on who you know and who is good for you if you are a 4/6- celebrate and include them (without trying to be likable).

Stand strong in your opinions, 4/1. You know your TRUTH.

Describe or demonstrate your unique process 2/4, 2/5. Forget about "them" for a minute - it is ALL about you.

Trust your natural magnetism, 3/5, and use humour to reframe your self-criticism (or that of others).

Dive into and share about your research, 1/4.

Play with life and tell us what you have discovered that is not working on 3/6 and 6/3.

**Secret #5: Do not be afraid to experiment.**

Your Human Design is unique, and it may take some trial and error to find what works best for you and your business.

There is no set-in-stone one way to make it work, and at the end of the day, you have to feel good about specific tactics and activities you are engaging with. The more aligned and in the flow that you feel - the better and more compelling your content becomes, and your magnetism opens up to great manifestations.

# Chapter Thirty-One

# Artifical Intelligence - Worth It?

## ChatGPT For Content Generation – get it right!

Before I move on, I want to address the idolisation of AI and all sorts of misunderstandings around it. It has taken the world by storm this year, and I see how often the excitement and ideas of easily generating great content can be so seductive. Yet, it is just **another form of conditioning** when we believe that something else can express what we have to say better than us. This is a belief I have been de-conditioning from intensively, and my mission is to give you a nutshell of how ChatGPT and other language-based AI models work. My goal is to empower you to lean into your gifts. Expressing them through content becomes so much more fluent with practice.

I did not fancy myself as a writer until I caught myself as I typing a very long post on Facebook. Suddenly, I felt this yummy taste in my mouth as I thought, "Ooooh, this is GOOD!" With this thought, I realised how much better a writer I already was – compared to how much credit I was willing to give myself for it. We often are so much better when we express ourselves from the heart, energetically lit up, not trying to say "what they need to hear".

But with the fast-growing popularity of tools that sounds so bloody convincing (at first) – there is a huge temptation to give your power away and watch it spit perfect-looking text in seconds, saving you lots of brain space and energy. And this is where the danger happens.

It is exactly the same reason why we struggle to focus when consuming digital materials. Our brains are always so overloaded with information, notifications, stuff on the sidebars, and taps open, to name just a few things. And then there are cute puppy reels... And this is so so confusing for the brain, which is a million-year-old evolving creation that is much slower in realising that there is no imminent danger of a sabre-toothed tiger jumping out of the bushes and killing us any second of the day. So the brain switches into survival mode, which means it is very careful where it allows the calorie burn. Watching, thinking, processing, creating burns so many calories, and in that overwhelming moment, the brain refuses to allow it.

This is why we feel reluctant to work hard, easily turning into anything that will "make our lives easier", and now the 21st century is giving us "the future" – AI-based writing tools. Naturally, the excitement and adoration go through the roof.

I am not a hater. I did as well fall into that trap. A LOT! In fact, I had generated a few bits for this book at the start too. It felt so awesome. I was giving "so much value"... Only to end up deleting EVERYTHING AI generated during the edit of the first draft. You see, after a little break from being elated with the results, I saw clearly how bland, wrong, and off-point it was, even when it gave me perfectly formed sentences. And I was very frustrated with myself because I was told by influencive people that "you can train" Chat GPT to give you exactly what you need. I ended up feeling stupid for not being able to train it. Thankfully... my daughter, Chantelle, mentioned a video she saw that explained exactly what ChatGPT is designed to do, and it became so clear to me what it can be used for and where we should NEVER allow its input. If you are interested, search for a video called "ChatGPT Explained Completely" by a quirky gamer called Kyle Hill. But to save you time, I will give you a very bottom-line explanation right here.

ChatGPT, known as a Narrow AI, is the most common kind of AI today. It has been around for decades. You use some form of Narrow AI on your phone alone daily. As the name suggests, this AI is designed to be highly focused on one single task or set of tasks, with some optimization and tweaking allowed. It is also considered "weak" AI because it cannot do anything else outside the designed task. So what is the task that ChatGPT and similar tools are performing?

In a few words: all it does is match a sequence of words based on how probable they would be used together in the desired context. Every time it accesses a massive database of WORDS uploaded based on everything digitalized before a date in 2021 (for Chat GPT), books, articles, and other internet content. Let me emphasise not information – only WORDS. So this AI does not understand or even know it is giving information because all it is doing is calculating the best "sounding" sequence of words to complete the task based on your prompt.

It does not go "search on the internet". It does not even search for the answer in the database – simply because its task is to match the most probable used words to create the output. This is why it sounds so convincing. EVEN when the output says, "I researched on the internet" or "I searched through my database", the AI does not even know it is saying that to you. Those are simply commonly put words to start a sentence, especially if you ask it a question. The difficulty is that often the outputs do sound like legitimate replies...

What does this mean?

All you can rely on in the output is word order. NOT the meaning, not the information, not facts. Any "correct" answers are purely coincidental. It does not know what "information" is. It only knows how to put together a sentence based on how commonly probable that specific words complete the sentence.

Let this sink in because when it did for me – I suddenly knew exactly where I could use the AI and where I do not want to go near it. For example, If I want to tell you why I do not recommend generating your content with AI if you feel you may not sound so good, I would write it myself. I want to make a point and express my perspective on what I have discovered.

YES, I am a 1/3 - "an expert on what does NOT work" – and this is such a juicy case to present. I tried it, deep dove in, got overexcited and gave it my power, only to find inconsistencies in the output that I could not ignore. And then I jumped into another rabbit hole, trying to prove my suspicions wrong if I was wrong. Only to find that video that put all the dots in their places.

And I also found a great use for such tools. Without expecting it to know anything. Because, in fact, **it is an awesome Narrow AI to work with language.**

For example, when I do a launch, I can record a series of videos and then ask Chat GPT to give me some suggestions on an email series. I tell it what tone I want it to be. I describe in detail what I said in each video. And then, it helps me generate an email that I can tweak and customize before adding to my launch schedule. Here is a secret: I never use ChatGPT to generate my social media posts where I want to express a point or nurture any sort of mindset-shifting, educating or nurturing content. This is MY EXPERTISE, and this is what people consume before they choose to work with me.

But I absolutely use AI to generate promotional blurbs for my articles and podcast episodes, launch emails – anything that just informs about something (like a new video, my new collaborations, or even an email about this book can easily be in parts generated by AI). I can ask it to summarise a longer text I wrote – but again, I need to be careful not to distort the context. The output always sounds so convincing it is easy not to question if it actually delivered a good takeaway or summary from what you wrote in the first place.

When it comes to my podcast episodes, I found that asking ChatGPT to summarise my transcript does not generate consistently good results. Often it misses the point because the text represents how humans talk, and some things are implied or unclear to it, so it just goes back to generating the most probable words and completely loses the plot. When I tried to summarise my Visibility By Design interview with Mari Smith (A Premier Facebook Marketing Expert and an influencer well-known in the world of marketing since 2007), the output suggested she was a small business owner struggling to market her business online. I rest my case. But at the same time, it was very decent generating possible titles for my episodes and even a pretty wonderful thank you note for my guests. So there are brilliant options where such tools are genuinely handy to save time and energy. And uses where AI is harmful to your credibility. The choice is yours, but I feel at peace now, having educated and warned you so that you can make an empowered one.

# To Wrap It Up: Epilogue

It can be difficult to navigate the world of business and marketing, but understanding your unique strategy and waiting for the right opportunities can absolutely lead to success. Regardless of the specifics, **your Human Design can not let you down.** When you trust it – you learn not to force yourself into opportunities that don't feel right. You attract the right people and opportunities that lead to success in all your endeavours. The universe will guide you to where you are meant to be. At the exact time when you are meant to be there. All you have to do is relax into it. And following your Strategy and Authority does indeed feel very relaxing!

Throughout this book, I mentioned a link to where you can access more resources and **order your personalised Marketing Blueprint By Design™ report – you can find it all at marketingbyhumandesign.com**. If you do, I hope to see you in person and dive deeper into how you can apply your Human Design strengths and gifts in your online visibility with ease so you feel harmony and joy showing up in your business.

On a personal note, as a woman approaching my Chiron return in 2027 (a magical landmark) with a star of visibility shining bright, I am only at the start of a mission to empower, maybe even millions, to spot and let go of their conditioning. No matter how scary it may seem at the start. I want to inspire them to embrace much more harmony and ease as they discover that what was holding them back so much is, in fact, powerless. Or, at the very least, help them find reliable tools and systems to walk past their fears and insecurities, follow their Authority, and master their Human Design Strategy. Step by step. Day by day.

It is an experiment – the only rule is that you observe and take responsibility for your own journey in this life – your decisions, whether they are made out of alignment or out of Not Self... Both are fine, of course. Your experience in this human form is a series of lessons that living on the material plane naturally present. And as a human, there is no such thing as perfection or full alignment. Experiment with your imperfection -in life, your business, your relationships – and Human Design merely shows you how living out your True Potential can be so much more fulfilling.

As for me, I think the awareness of my Design is the reason my life did not fall apart since losing my dear husband and the love of my life, Les Stapleton, no matter how bad it hurts. The pain I use as a springboard to writing this book, and this is only the beginning of something beautiful.

In fact, there is too much in the bodygraph, indicating that perhaps I will enjoy this new chapter of my life more than I have ever expected. Everything is happening just how it is meant to happen so I can live out my True Potential... And I instinctively sense it already.

I open my arms widely to embrace what the future holds.

I am surrounded by incredible people who see and recognise me, who fully support me and cheer me on.

I feel loved, blessed and excited. Thank you for sharing this journey with me.

# Acknowledgements

This book is dedicated to my late husband Les, an extraordinary figure in many's lives, who fully devoted himself to me until his very last breath. To my daughter Chantelle, whose mom I am so proud to be (no matter how unconventional, goofy and neuro-spicy I get, she keeps up with me in all states), she is my world. To my mom, a great teacher in my life. My little sister Benita who stood by me in these hardest times of my life, and whom I love so dearly. My close family who gave me the space I so desperately needed and did not choke me to despair with unnecessary sympathies. To my true friend through the decades, Nataly Hunt, who fought for me when I was paralysed with fear and grief.

To Marian McKenna, my dear friend, Fairy God Mother, soul sister and a woman whom I deeply admire and am inspired by on so many levels and who has shown me so much love and support for over a decade. I treasure our connection.

A very special thank you to Mari Smith for representing "the door that opens" when I felt the other door was slamming shut in a debilitatingly slow way during my husband's last weeks. Ever since I followed you in 2007, I have felt so strongly connected, but little did I know that we were meant to leave a mark on each other's journey and that we would be collaborating on this book, which is probably the most prominent piece I have published to date. Your presence on my journey is the Universe saying: **nothing is impossible when you trust the flow.**

To Monique Alvarez, the founder of AMA Publishing, who so generously supported and guided me through the launch of this book and whose incredible influence has made it a success.

To Louise Wilson, a very special conscious vitality coach, who has been with me every step of my husband's final journey, working with our energy in the domain invisible to the human eye and helping us connect and get closure while we still could. Thanks to you, when the time came, I was as ready as I could be, and you knew exactly what I needed to to help us both with this transition. I will never forget your incredible, special support.

I want to say thank you for your incredible loyalty, support, and love and for "seeing me" to all my Visibility That Sells Accelerator members and my private clients. You know who you are. Every call we spend together is inspiring, deeply healing and transformational. To all my one-off Marketing Blueprint By Design™ clients – thank you for bringing me such unique opportunities to look into you, to see and guide you, and to inspire you to express your unique magical selves. I always feel I only attract my ideal people, and you guys are the evidence that it is absolutely true.

To my accountant partner Melina Ali from Money Matters, who is so much more than an excellent expert in the realm of pure confusion (numbers) but also a sensitive and caring person with a huge heart. I am so grateful we met and are still to ACTUALLY meet! (Oh, the joys of online entrepreneurship!)

To my book coach Kate Oman for holding space for me, motivating and encouraging me throughout the book writing process.

To a beautiful photoshoot team Larissa Kogan (Medieval.photo) & make-up artist Maryna Olkhovska (@dubchukmakeup)

Throughout the book, I make some references to specific works that inspired me:

"An A to D of You: The Human Design System." by Richard Rudd

"Understanding Your Clients through Human Design. The Breakthrough Technology." by Robin Winn, MFT

"Understanding The Centers In Human Design. The Facilitator's Guide To Transforming Pain Into Possibility." by Robin Winn, MFT

"The 64 Material Ways" Ra Uru Hu (www.JovianArchive.com ©Jovian Archive Media.)

# *What they say...*

"Juliette is a magician. She helped me understand my profile in ways no one had been able to in the last four years I've been researching. I printed off her report and read it regularly. Her video walkthrough is so incredibly spot-on. It's unreal! I also referred many of my clients to her. I can't imagine being in life and business without a clear understanding of who we are, how others relate to us, and how we thrive. I can't recommend her enough!"

***Monique Alvarez, USA Today Bestselling Author & Founder of AMA Publishing,*** **Emotional Manifesting Generator 5/1** https://amapublishing.co/

"Finally, a truly personalized approach to marketing! In just a few months of working with Juliette, I finally feel like I've come home to myself with my marketing. Despite all my knowledge of Human Design, I hadn't been able to find my groove because I kept listening to the "experts" rather than my inner self. Starting with my Marketing Blueprint, I felt an instant recognition, and I've continued that in her visibility by design program. This really works! In less than two months, I've already gotten far more confident in my writing on social media, and the shift in magnetic attraction is concrete - for the first time ever, I got over 2800 views on a LinkedIn post. Juliette truly is an amazing mentor and guide, balancing accountability with support and very practical implementation strategies that enable me to truly align with my design."

***Dr. Bobbi Kline, Founder Integrative Personalized Medicine -*** **Self-Projected Projector 5/1** https://bobbiklinemd.com

"As someone totally new to marketing, I'd spent two years taking all the courses that popped up on my feed and following all the instructions I was given on what I should be doing to build my coaching business. All that happened was I felt increasingly frustrated that nothing was working and that what I was being told to do was making me really uncomfortable. One call with Juliette and it was like a weight falling off my shoulders, and I finally understood why 'the standard practice' wasn't working for me and felt so icky when I tried to do it. I came away from that call with a clear focus on how to move forward and signed up on the spot to work with Juliette for a year. Four months in, and everything has shifted... I'm enjoying marketing in a way that's comfortable for me and, more importantly, is actually working!"

***Rachel Franke, Mindset & Diet Coach*** **Emotional Generator 2/4** https://rachelfcoaching.com

"Working with you has given me the confidence to be and trust myself, both in building my business and marketing. I now know there is no 'one size fits all, I have to do it my way, and there are no 'shoulds' anymore. You helped me give myself permission to be me.

I used to think I needed to have something grand to say every time in every post. Some world-changing deep thought or insight. Because of my specific Human Design and your coaching on this, I now know I have just to be myself and share what I'm doing. That is the way I bring my light into this world. And this is what feels true and authentic. This has changed the way I perceive my marketing. It's now all about connection and being true to myself. No shoulds!"

***Maartje de Boer, Artist*** – **Emotional Manifesting Generator 2/4** https://madebo.art/

"We need more Juliettes in the world! She brings such enthusiasm and natural spontaneity to her private coaching calls. One can just feel her honesty and integrity when working with her. And it's this which encourages us to take a bigger step in our own visibility. I love how she sees through the 'cracks' of our own make-up with her outstanding knowledge of Human Design and gently steers us to understand a lot more about how we operate naturally and to be ok to work with our particular design. Her mission to help people get who they are and how they process, at their core level, whether in personal or business, will go a long way to spreading acceptance, encouragement and confidence in the individual to share their talents in the world."

***Louise Wilson, Conscious Vitality Coach*** – **Pure Manifesting Generator 5/1** https://heilahealth.co.za/

Juliette helped me debunk traditional marketing and develop a marketing style that resonated with me. She inspired me to be more direct in my messaging and challenge the status quo that had limited me for so long. I tended to hide behind the information. Juliette would take my message, and with a tweak here and a word change there, my words became a simple and clear reflection of what I wanted to say. She helped me work with my "invisible" and trust that sharing my natural voice is plenty. She transformed a process (marketing) which felt like pulling teeth to me into a fun and inspiring experience and taught me to market when inspired and not because I should - this was a game changer for me.

***Annita Keane, Prosperity Coach,*** **Emotional Projector 5/1** http s://thekeanemethod.com

"I am so energized (and relieved!) by what Juliette's unique report and discussion enabled me to both discover and do – not only did her fresh perspective validate information about myself and what I'm destined to create, it got me over the major mental blocks I've been experiencing forever in launching my business, and I just confidently took a significant step! She helped me understand how to better align my purpose and style in the practical and meaningful way that I've been yearning for; it made so much sense and felt incredible. Given authenticity is part of my personal brand, this was absolutely perfect. Juliette is so authentically fun and inspiring to work with! I find myself referring to my Blueprint report often, to keep me focused, inspired and energetically aligned."

***Amy Hooper Hanna CEO, AhHA! Leadership coach, Communication Strategist, Speaker, Facilitator, Author,*** E***motional***

***Manifesting Generator 1/3*** https://www.ahha-consulting.com

"Juliette has provided me with clarity and confidence in following the inner direction I feel toward marketing my services. With so little expertise of my own, I've tried to follow what seems like various best practices but have yet to find my groove in that. I feel I now have sound advice, a few key pointers to follow, and a direction for my natural expression."

***Sandra Lyne, Guide to Spiritual Awakening*** - **Self-Projected Projector 5/1** https://sandralyne.com/

"My Incarnation Cross (life purpose) is literally about masks, expressing my leadership through a flexible identity...so I have always had trouble expressing my essence, defining which of them is my brand. I'm so glad the universe put Juliette in my path when it did... she helped me cut through the confusion and complexity and take ownership of my 1000-mile perspective, which used to alienate people. Now I am letting my type and profile do the talking and aligning with what other people see in me—someone who universalizes information & helps the world walk in a new paradigm. I am here to share my stories, ideas, and insights. It really is just that simple!"

***Kristen Caven, Literary Creative & Consultant,*** **Mental Projector 5/2** https://kristencaven.com

"Juliette is the guide that inspired my biggest aha's! "Projectors don't push, but they must be visible. Waiting is being active; we only need an invitation to give direct advice. Focus on the things you love and get immersed in that. When you are in that zone, you are aligned and magnetic. Approach social media when you have something to say." This advice is brilliant and feels great to me. I have been told so many things by so many "experts", yet this insight is truly going to change my marketing because it is very aligned with who I am."

***Angela Legh, Author of the Bella Santini Chronicles,*** **Emotional Projector 1/3** https://angelalegh.com/

## What's next?

**For more of my online visibility guidance, order your personalised Marketing Blueprint By Design™ report – you can find it all at marketingbyhumandesign.com**

You can also **invite me to speak on the topics discussed in this book on your podcast or in your community** – visit https://juliettestapleton.com/media

Your Guide, Juliette

Printed in Great Britain
by Amazon

45778251R00149